Bonne Maman®

The Seasonal Cookbook

Bonne Maman®

The Seasonal Cookbook

Inspirational recipes using conserves and compotes

SIMON &
SCHUSTER

London · New York · Sydney · Toronto

A CBS COMPANY

Acknowledgements

Bonne Maman would like to thank Aga for the use
of the recipes on pages 14, 30, 42, 50, 80, 86, 108,
114, 130 and 174.

PICTURE ACKNOWLEDGEMENTS:
Page 6: Remko Kraaijeveld
Page 9: Photolibrary/FoodCollection.
Page 19: Simon Bevan
Page 53: GAP Photos/Paul Debois.
Page 97: Photolibrary/Radius Images.
Page 141: Photolibrary/Garden Picture Library/
    Pernilla Bergdahl.

First published in Great Britain by
Simon & Schuster UK Ltd., 2011
A CBS Company

Design Copyright © Simon & Schuster
Illustrated Books 2011
Text and Photography Copyright ©
Andros SNC 2011

SIMON & SCHUSTER
ILLUSTRATED BOOKS
Simon & Schuster UK
222 Gray's Inn Road
London WC1X 8HB
www.simonandschuster.co.uk

A CIP catalogue record of this book is available
from the British Library.

10 9 8 7 6 5 4 3 2 1

Editorial Director: Francine Lawrence
Managing Editor: Nicky Hill
Project Editor: Abi Waters
Design: Geoff Fennell
Production Manager: Katherine Thornton
Photography: Myles New
Recipe Development and Food Styling:
    Moyra Fraser
Art Direction and Styling: Tony Hutchinson

Printed and bound in Singapore

ISBN 978-0-85720-209-3
ISBN 978-0-85720-210-9 (Corporate edition)

Contents

la belle vie avec
Bonne Maman ®

A byword for style and quality, Bonne Maman has held pride of place on breakfast tables for many decades. The rich fruity conserves, tangy marmalades and delectable compotes evoke the warmth of a Provençal summer even on the coldest of winter days. Using generous amounts of sweet, fragrant fruits and simply cooked with natural and cane sugars, each jar is redolent of the traditional art of making conserves.

Thickly spread onto warm buttery croissants, lavishly heaped on hot toasted brioche, stirred into a bowl of creamy yogurt or generously added to a piece of freshly baked baguette, Bonne Maman's indulgent conserves are the epitome of good taste. And who could fail to love the nostalgia of a really good conserve at tea-time, be it on freshly baked scones or spread in a classic Victoria sponge cake?

But now Bonne Maman is also a larder staple for the discerning cook. Adding conserve to a recipe gives depth of flavour: a couple of spoonfuls of Berries and Cherries Conserve swirled into a creamy syllabub, enriching a pork casserole with Peach Conserve or adding Strawberry Conserve to the dressing for a confit of duck salad – this is exciting cuisine.

This book is for all year round inspiration. Divided into seasons, each section has recipes and craft ideas that reflect the time of year. Foods have been chosen when they are at their best and are used in a series of innovative and delicious recipes that give weekday suppers and weekend entertaining extra panache. From chic soups, fragrant fish, heart-warming stews and elegant vegetables to mouth-watering desserts, gorgeous cakes, amazing picnic foods and stunning salads, this is fabulous food that combines tradition with a contemporary twist. And all made with a little Bonne Maman magic.

In addition, many recipes are accompanied by one or two 'Cook's Tips': handy hints and alternative flavour suggestions designed to make time in the kitchen even more enjoyable.

Few can resist the Bonne Maman jar; the timeless design, handwritten labels and iconic gingham lids owe their desirability to sheer simplicity. There are so many different ways they can be used, providing practical storage solutions while adding a flourish of French country chic. There are plenty of inspiring suggestions included in the book for using the stylish jars: mini pots made into a unique Advent Calendar, novel packaging for homemade gifts and a picnic container for chilled soup are just a few of the beautifully illustrated, original craft ideas.

So, not just the best conserve for breakfast but an integral part of every cook's larder and every hospitable home. Welcome to 'la belle vie' with Bonne Maman.

printemps
spring

Creamed Tomato and Orange Soup with Fresh Crab Croutes

This soup has such a simple but delicious blend of flavours – and it can be made in advance, which is always useful. The marmalade adds a touch of sweet orange and tempers the acidity of the tomatoes perfectly.

Serves 6–8

ingredients

50 g (2 oz) butter

2 tbsp olive oil

4 small red onions, roughly chopped

2 celery sticks, finely chopped

450 g (1 lb) butternut squash, peeled and chopped

3 fat garlic cloves

2–3 tbsp Bonne Maman Bitter Orange Marmalade

2 x 400 g tins chopped tomatoes with chilli

600 ml (1 pint) chicken or vegetable stock

1 x 150 ml carton single cream

Salt and freshly ground black pepper

to finish

1 small ciabatta loaf, thinly sliced and toasted

2 tbsp finely chopped fresh parsley

A few strips of red chilli or pepper

75 g (3 oz) fresh white crab meat

method

In a large saucepan melt the butter and 1 tablespoon of the oil and fry the onion, celery, squash and 2 of the garlic cloves for 7–10 minutes, or until the onion is very soft and golden.

Stir in the marmalade, tomatoes and stock. Bring to the boil and simmer for 30–35 minutes until all the vegetables are tender.

Cool and then liquidise the soup in a food processor or blender or with a hand-held blender. Stir in the cream, adjust the seasoning and return to the saucepan to reheat gently.

Brush the ciabatta toasts with the remaining olive oil and garlic clove. Stir the parsley and chilli or pepper into the crab meat and fork a little onto each ciabatta toast. Top each bowl of soup with some crab croutes before serving.

COOK'S TIPS

* This soup can be made up to 3 days ahead. It also freezes well.
* Spread the toasts lightly with a creamy garlic mayonnaise for an extra garlic 'kick'.
* As an alternative to fresh crab, spread the toasts with soft goats' cheese or coarsely grated Gruyère.

Buckwheat Pancakes with Goats' Cheese and Sweet Roasted Squash

Pancakes are usually associated with sweet recipes, but these buckwheat pancakes are perfectly matched with creamy cheese and golden squash.

Serves 6

ingredients

1 butternut squash, peeled and chopped
6–8 garlic cloves, thinly sliced
1 tbsp pine nuts
4 tbsp Bonne Maman Apricot Conserve
2 tbsp olive oil
2 tbsp lemon juice
4 tbsp fresh orange juice
A knob of butter, for greasing
225 g (8 oz) soft, fresh goats' cheese
2 tbsp roughly chopped mixed fresh mint and parsley

for the pancake batter

25 g (1 oz) buckwheat flour
60 g (2½ oz) strong white plain flour
A large pinch of salt
½ tsp easy-blend dried yeast
1 egg, separated
75 ml (3 fl oz) crème fraîche
100 ml (3½ fl oz) whole milk, warmed
15 g (½ oz) butter, melted

method

Mix together all the dry pancake batter ingredients in a large bowl.

Whisk the egg yolk and crème fraîche into the milk in a separate bowl and beat into the dry ingredients to form a thick batter. Cover and leave in a warm place for about 1 hour.

In a clean bowl, whisk the egg white until stiff, then fold into the batter. Cover and leave for another hour.

Meanwhile, preheat the oven to 200°C (fan oven 180°C), gas mark 6.

Put the squash, garlic and pine nuts in a roasting tin. Whisk together the conserve, olive oil, lemon juice and orange juice, then stir half the mixture into the squash and garlic. Roast in the preheated oven for 35–40 minutes until golden, then stir in the remaining apricot mixture.

Heat a small non-stick frying pan and brush lightly with butter. Pour in about 2 tablespoons of the batter and swirl around the pan to make a thin layer about 10 cm (4 inches) round. Leave to cook for about 40 seconds before flipping and cooking for a further 40 seconds. Tip onto a plate and keep warm while you continue with the remaining batter.

Put 6 pancakes on an edged baking sheet and spread with the goats' cheese. Pop under a hot grill until golden.

Spoon over the roasted butternut squash, then serve finished with the chopped herbs.

Grilled Mackerel with Rhubarb Sauce

These fresh mackerels would also be great grilled on the barbecue to make the most of any super-hot spring evenings.

Serves 6

ingredients

6 fresh mackerel, weighing
   about 225 g (8 oz) each, gutted
   and cleaned
1 lemon, cut into 12 half-slices
15 g (½ oz) butter, melted
Salt and freshly ground black
   pepper
1 tbsp chopped fresh parsley

for the sauce

9 tbsp Bonne Maman Rhubarb
   Compote
Zest and juice of 1½ unwaxed
   lemons
3 tbsp white wine vinegar
1 cm (½ inch) piece of fresh
   ginger, peeled and sliced
Salt and ground white pepper

method

Put all the sauce ingredients in a stainless steel saucepan and heat gently over a low heat for 3–5 minutes, until combined and reduced to a coating consistency. Remove from the heat, discard the ginger and allow to cool.

Preheat the grill to a high heat.

Pat the mackerel dry with kitchen paper. Make 2 or 3 deep slashes in the side of each fish and lightly season the cavities; add 2 half-slices of lemon to each fish.

Place the mackerel in a shallow roasting tin or on an edged baking sheet. Brush both sides with melted butter and season lightly.

Reduce the grill to a medium heat and cook the fish placed 5–7.5 cm (2–3 inches) from the heat source for 6–8 minutes, then turn over and grill the other side. Serve sprinkled with the chopped parsley and with the warm rhubarb sauce.

COOK'S TIPS

* If cooking the mackerel on a barbecue, use a fish rack to make turning the fish easier.
* Omit the lemon and use slices of fresh orange.

Baked Beetroot Salad with Feta and Pine Nuts

The earthy richness of the vegetable patch mixed with a hint of Mediterranean sunshine come together in this fresh-tasting salad.

Serves 4

ingredients

3 raw beetroot
3 tbsp balsamic vinegar
3 tbsp Bonne Maman Berries
  and Cherries Conserve
Finely grated zest from
  ½ orange, plus the juice
  of 1 orange
1 bay leaf
A few sprigs of fresh thyme, plus
  extra to finish
125 g (4 oz) feta cheese
25 g (1 oz) toasted pine nuts
Salt and freshly ground black
  pepper

method

Preheat the oven to 200°C (fan oven 180°C), gas mark 6.

Trim the beetroot greens away, being careful not to pierce the skin. Scrub the beetroot and wrap them in foil. Bake in the preheated oven for 1–2 hours or until tender (check them towards the end of the cooking time as the timing depends on the age and size of the beetroot).

Meanwhile, place the balsamic vinegar, conserve, orange zest and juice, bay leaf and thyme in a saucepan with a pinch of salt and some freshly ground black pepper.

Heat gently and simmer for 5 minutes, then remove from the heat and set aside to allow the flavours to infuse.

When cool enough to handle, peel the skins from the cooked beetroots and trim the roots. Thinly slice and arrange on a large flat serving dish, overlapping the slices.

Sieve the lukewarm sauce, then drizzle it over the beetroot slices and put to one side for about 1 hour to allow the beetroot to absorb the flavours.

Just before serving, crumble the feta cheese over the beetroot, then sprinkle with the toasted pine nuts and a few fresh thyme leaves.

COOK'S TIPS
* The cooked beetroot can be left to marinate in the sauce overnight in a cool room for added flavour.
* Serve as part of a buffet, with cold meats and some crusty French bread to mop up the juices.

Roast Chicken with Cherry Couscous Stuffing

Couscous offers a lighter alternative to traditional breadcrumbs in this sweet herby stuffing. Combined with tender roast chicken it makes a supper that's more than good enough to share with friends.

Serves 4

ingredients

150 g (5 oz) Bonne Maman
    Cherry Compote
50 g (2 oz) couscous
1 small red onion, finely
    chopped
2 tbsp olive oil
4 spring onions, roughly
    chopped
2 tbsp each of chopped fresh
    thyme and parsley
Grated zest and juice of 1 small
    orange
1 free-range chicken, weighing
    about 1.4 kg (3 lb)
300 ml (½ pint) chicken or
    vegetable stock
1 tbsp butter, softened
2 tbsp plain flour
Salt and freshly ground black
    pepper

method

Spoon the compote into a mesh sieve over a small bowl and spread out the fruit. Leave to drain for about 1 hour.

Put the couscous in a small bowl and pour over enough cold water to come 2.5 cm (1 inch) above the level of the grains. Set aside for 15 minutes.

Meanwhile, fry the red onion in half the oil for 5–7 minutes or until soft and golden. Add the spring onions, then remove from the heat, stir in the herbs and orange zest and cool.

Preheat the oven to 190°C (fan oven 170°C), gas mark 5.

Fork the drained cherries (reserving the juice) and cold onion mixture into the couscous and season well. Spoon the stuffing into the neck end of the chicken, fold over the flap of skin and secure with a wooden cocktail stick.

Sit the chicken in a roasting tin just large enough to hold it comfortably and pour the stock around the base. Brush the chicken with the remaining oil and spread the breast with the butter. Season well.

Cook in the preheated oven, basting every 20 minutes, for about 1¼ hours. To test if it is cooked, pierce the thigh meat with a skewer and the juices should run clear.

Lift the chicken onto a serving dish, cover loosely with foil and keep warm. Pour all but 2 tablespoons of the cooking liquid into a jug and add the reserved cherry compote liquid.

Put the roasting tin over the hob and whisk in the flour. Cook over a medium heat until pale golden, then gradually whisk in the contents of the jug. Bring to the boil and bubble until reduced and lightly thickened. Add orange juice to taste and serve with the chicken and stuffing.

COOK'S TIPS

* Allow the cherries plenty of time to drain. The fruit should be quite 'dry' when it is stirred into the couscous.
* Try serving the chicken with steamed new potatoes that have been tossed with a little butter and a handful of chopped watercress.

Pretty and practical

It's very easy for the family sewing box to become muddled. Bonne Maman's handy jars make it much simpler to organise all the bits and bobs in an efficient and attractive way. Cotton reels, buttons, needles, tape measure, pieces of fabric and ribbon can all be tidied away and easily found.

Use a spare piece of your favourite material to make a colourful pin cushion to stick onto the lid of a jar and it becomes both functional and eye-catching at the same time!

Herby Lamb with Woodland Dressing

This is a really simple, small roast to serve for dinner. Lamb loin is the prime cut and can be expensive, but it is guaranteed to be tender, has no waste and is very simple to carve. You do need to keep an eye on the clock so you don't overcook it.

Serves 6

ingredients

3 small lamb loin fillets,
   weighing about 350 g
   (12 oz) each
3 tbsp Bonne Maman Woodland
   Berries Conserve
9 slices Parma ham
3 sprigs each of fresh thyme and
   rosemary
3 tbsp balsamic glaze
2 fat garlic cloves, thinly sliced
3 tbsp olive oil
150 ml (¼ pint) chicken or
   vegetable stock
225 g (8 oz) tiny cherry
   tomatoes

method

Brush the lamb fillets all over with 1 tablespoon of the conserve. Wrap each fillet in 3 slices of Parma ham. Lay a sprig of thyme and a sprig of rosemary on each fillet and tie at intervals with fine string to secure.

Whisk together the remaining conserve with the balsamic glaze, the garlic and 2 tablespoons of the olive oil. Put the lamb fillets in a bowl and cover with the conserve mixture. Cover and leave to marinate in the fridge overnight.

Preheat the oven to 220°C (fan oven 200°C), gas mark 7.

Lift the lamb fillets from the marinade, brushing off any excess (reserve the marinade for later). Heat the remaining oil in a small roasting tin on the hob and brown the fillets quickly on all sides.

Pour about 50 ml (2 fl oz) of stock into the base of the tin and transfer to the preheated oven for about 12 minutes for medium rare (adjust the cooking time for rare or well done).

Remove the lamb from the oven, lift from the tin, cover with foil and set aside to rest.

Put the roasting tin back over the hob and stir in the tomatoes, the reserved marinade from earlier and the remaining stock. Bring to the boil and bubble for about 2–3 minutes until thickened and syrupy.

Remove the string from the fillets and serve the lamb cut into thick slices, drizzled with the warm sauce.

COOK'S TIPS

* The lamb is wonderful served on a bed of creamy mashed potato mixed with peas and accompanied by fresh green vegetables.
* Use tiny button mushrooms as an alternative to the tomatoes.

Bobotie

All self-respecting South African housewives own and treasure a favourite Bobotie recipe. It is quite similar to the traditional shepherd's pie but lightly spiced with a baked egg and yogurt topping.

Serves 4

ingredients

25 g (1 oz) butter

1 large onion, finely chopped

2 garlic cloves, crushed

2.5 cm (1 inch) piece of fresh
   ginger, peeled and grated

1 tbsp garam masala

2 bay leaves

2 tsp ground turmeric

400 g (14 oz) minced beef

4 tbsp Bonne Maman Apricot
   Conserve

300 ml (½ pint) chicken or
   vegetable stock

3 tbsp chopped fresh parsley

Salt and freshly ground black
   pepper

for the topping

150 g (5 oz) Greek yogurt

100 ml (3½ fl oz) milk

2 large eggs

method

Preheat the oven to 180°C (fan oven 160°C), gas mark 4.

Melt the butter in a saucepan and cook the onion and garlic until soft and golden. Stir in the ginger, garam masala, bay leaves and all but a pinch of the turmeric. Cook, stirring, for 3–4 minutes, then remove from the pan using a slotted spoon.

Put the minced beef into the pan and fry, without any oil, until a deep golden brown. Return the onions to the pan along with the conserve and stock. Bring to the boil, then simmer, uncovered, for 20 minutes or until most of the stock has been absorbed and the beef is quite dry.

Stir in the parsley and season. Spoon the mixture into a shallow ovenproof dish and leave to cool.

For the topping, whisk together the yogurt, milk and eggs with the remaining pinch of turmeric. Season, then spoon over the meat. It will sink down into the meat a little but don't worry.

Cook in the preheated oven for 25–30 minutes or until the topping has set and is golden brown.

COOK'S TIPS

* The mince mixture without the topping will freeze well.
* Make half the mixture and spoon into scooped out baked potatoes, add the topping and bake for 15–20 minutes.
* Serve this great family supper with a fruity chutney and green salad.

Confit of Duck Salad
with New Season Asparagus

Confit is the French word for preserve and is a wonderful way of serving duck if you like it with a crisp, crunchy skin.

**Serves 6 as a starter
or 3 for lunch**

ingredients

225 g (8 oz) asparagus, trimmed
2 confit of duck legs
75 g (3 oz) pea shoots or soft
  baby salad leaves
Salt and freshly ground black
  pepper

for the dressing

1 sprig of fresh rosemary
9 tbsp extra virgin olive oil
2 pink shallots, finely diced
2 garlic cloves, sliced
5 tbsp Bonne Maman Strawberry
  Conserve
3–4 tbsp sherry vinegar

method

First, make the dressing. Remove the leaves from the sprig of rosemary and finely chop them (reserving the stalk). Heat 3 tablespoons of the olive oil in a frying pan and cook the shallots and garlic with the rosemary leaves for 2–3 minutes until it begins to sizzle and turn golden brown.

Remove from the heat, stir in the remaining oil, the conserve and the vinegar. Season the dressing and pour into an empty jar. Push in the reserved rosemary stalk, seal and leave to marinate in a cool place for at least 24 hours or up to 1 week (the longer the better).

Cook the asparagus in plenty of boiling, salted water until just tender. Drain and immediately plunge into ice-cold water to cool. Drain and keep chilled until needed.

About 2 hours before serving, preheat the oven to 220°C (fan oven 200°C), gas mark 7.

Cook the confit of duck legs in the preheated oven for about 15 minutes or until golden brown and crispy. Remove from the oven, set aside to cool, then shred the meat from the bones. Spoon 2–3 tablespoons of dressing over the warm duck meat.

When ready to serve, divide the asparagus between 6 serving plates. Top with the shredded duck and some pea shoots or salad leaves. Spoon over a little extra dressing before serving.

COOK'S TIPS

* The dressing is also wonderful served with smoked meats and salty, soft goats' cheese.
* If you cannot find confit of duck, poach 2 duck legs gently in stock for 1 hour until very tender. Drain well, rub the skin with a little salt and olive oil and roast as above.

Crispy Crumbed Romano Peppers

Romano peppers are ideal for stuffing and roasting, which softens the flesh and concentrates their flavour. These peppers are finally coated in egg and breadcrumbs for an extra added crunch.

Serves 4

ingredients

2 large Spanish onions, finely
   chopped
25 g (1 oz) butter
4 tbsp Bonne Maman Wild
   Blueberry Conserve
2 tbsp capers, roughly chopped
4 tbsp tomato purée
2 x 200 g packs red Romano
   peppers (about 4 peppers)
2 eggs, beaten
125 g (4 oz) soft goats' cheese
8 tbsp dried white breadcrumbs

method

Preheat the oven to 200°C (fan oven 180°C), gas mark 6. Line an edged baking sheet with greaseproof paper.

Cook the onion slowly in the butter in a frying pan until very soft and golden – this should take a good 15 minutes. Stir in the conserve, capers and tomato purée. Leave to cool.

Make a slit along one side of each pepper and open out a little, remove any seeds and discard. Divide the onion mixture between the peppers. Beat about half the egg into the goats' cheese in a small bowl and then spoon this over the onion mixture.

Brush the peppers all over with the remaining egg and then pat with the breadcrumbs. Place the peppers on the prepared baking sheet.

Bake the peppers in the preheated oven for 20–25 minutes or until just tender and golden brown.

COOK'S TIP
* Look for large packs of Japanese Panko breadcrumbs in Asian supermarkets. They are a variety of flaky breadcrumb used in cooking as a crunchy coating for fried foods. Panko is made from bread without crusts, and it has a crisper, airier texture than most other dried crumbs.

Gardening the *Bonne Maman* way.

Venison Steaks with Blackcurrant Sauce

Venison steaks are perfect for a chilly spring evening when you are after a hearty meal – they are rich and delicious when accompanied by a deep, fruity sauce.

Serves 4

ingredients

4 venison steaks (or small medallions of fillet of beef), weighing about 125–150 g (4–5 oz) each
Olive oil, for brushing
Salt and freshly ground black pepper
Parsleyed sautéed potatoes, to finish

for the sauce

150 g (5 oz) Bonne Maman Blackcurrant Conserve
150 ml (¼ pint) port
1 tbsp red wine vinegar
Juice of ½ lemon

method

To make the sauce, place the blackcurrant conserve and port into a saucepan and bring to the boil. Add the vinegar and bubble to reduce for 5 minutes until the sauce has thickened slightly. Add the lemon juice and pepper to taste. Keep the sauce warm until needed.

Wipe the venison steaks with kitchen paper and brush lightly with olive oil. Season both sides and place into a hot griddle pan. Grill on both sides for 2–3 minutes, about 4–6 minutes in total, dependent upon the thickness of the steaks and how you like it cooked.

Serve on hot plates with the sauce poured over, accompanied by some parsleyed sautéed potatoes.

COOK'S TIPS

* The sauce can be made up to 2 days ahead and kept in a cool place. Reheat gently to serve.
* The same sauce is delicious with grilled lamb cutlets, venison sausages or roast duck.

Chicken, Prawn and Sweet Potato Curry

Inviting friends round for supper on a Friday evening? Make life easy for yourself with this quick curry. The confiture adds a delicious, rich sweetness to the dish similar to palm sugar. Serve the curry quite simply with warm naan bread, chutney, lime wedges and an onion and chopped mint salad.

Serves 6

ingredients

- 2 tbsp olive oil
- 2 onions, sliced
- 2 fat garlic cloves, crushed
- A large pinch of red chilli flakes or 1 tsp finely chopped red chilli
- 1 tbsp mild tikka curry powder
- 1 tsp ground turmeric
- 1 x 400 ml tin coconut milk
- 4 tbsp Bonne Maman Confiture de Caramel
- 2 tbsp smooth peanut butter
- 12 boned and skinned chicken thighs, cut into bite-sized pieces
- 3 small sweet potatoes, about 550 g (1¼ lb), peeled and roughly chopped
- 150 g (5 oz) cooked and peeled king prawns

method

Heat the oil in a wok or deep frying pan and cook the onion with the garlic until soft and pale golden. Stir in the red chilli, curry powder and turmeric and cook, stirring, for a further minute.

Add the coconut milk, confiture de caramel, peanut butter, chicken and sweet potato and bring to the boil. Reduce the heat until the mixture is gently simmering and leave to cook for about 10–12 minutes or until the chicken is cooked through and the potato is tender. Add a little water if the liquid becomes too thick.

Stir in the prawns and mix for 1 minute only so that the prawns are just heated through. Serve immediately.

COOK'S TIPS

* To prepare ahead, cook the curry without the prawns. Cool and chill overnight or freeze. To use, thaw the mixture, if necessary, and return to a gentle simmer. Simmer for 10–15 minutes until piping hot, adding extra water if necessary. Stir in the prawns as above.
* Garnish the curry with roughly chopped coriander or basil and some finely chopped roasted peanuts.
* For a vegetarian alternative, omit the chicken and prawns and add a drained 400 g tin chickpeas or kidney beans.

Roasted Pepper and Ricotta Pies

These little pies can be prepared entirely ahead of time. What makes them so special is the layers of cheese and roasted vegetables, blended with fig all encased in crispy pastry.

Makes 6

ingredients

1 red pepper and 1 orange pepper, deseeded and roughly chopped
2 garlic cloves, crushed
1 small red onion, roughly chopped
225 g (8 oz) courgettes, thinly sliced
3 tbsp olive oil
4 tbsp Bonne Maman Fig Conserve
1 x 500 g pack chilled puff pastry
Flour, for dusting
1 x 200 g tub ricotta cheese
50 g (2 oz) freshly grated Parmesan cheese
1 small egg, beaten
Freshly ground black pepper
Crisp, green salad, to finish

method

Preheat the oven to 200°C (fan oven 180°C), gas mark 6.

Put the peppers, garlic, onion and courgettes in a roasting tin and drizzle over the olive oil. Roast in the preheated oven for 25–30 minutes until soft and beginning to char round the edges. Stir the conserve into the warm vegetables and leave to cool.

Meanwhile, roll out about 200 g (7 oz) of the pastry very thinly on a lightly floured surface and place on a foil-lined baking sheet. The pastry should be about the same size as the sheet. Chill in the fridge for 30 minutes.

Prick all over with a fork and bake the chilled pastry in the oven above the vegetables for 10–12 minutes or until golden brown and cooked through.

Press the cooked pastry down to flatten it and stamp out 6 x 8.5 cm (3½ inch) rounds. Place on a fresh baking sheet.

Mix together the two cheeses and season with black pepper. Divide between the pastry bases, leaving a small edge of pastry clear. Top the cheese with the cold roasted vegetables.

Roll out the remaining pastry very thinly and stamp out 6 x 12 cm (5 inch) rounds. Brush the cooked pastry edge with beaten egg and cover the pie filling with the new pastry rounds. Tuck the excess pastry under the cooked bases, press down well and brush the pie tops with the remaining egg.

Cook in the oven for 15–20 minutes or until puffed and golden. Serve warm or cold with a crisp, green salad.

COOK'S TIPS

* The pies can be prepared up to the point that the complete pie is ready for the oven the day before and then chilled or frozen. To use, thaw overnight in the fridge, if necessary. Brush with a little extra beaten egg and bake as above.
* It may seem fiddly to cook the pastry bases beforehand but it makes the finished pies crispy all over.
* Omit the Parmesan cheese and use a mixture of half and half feta and ricotta cheese.

Chocolate and Strawberry Roulade

You will never have a more appreciative audience than when you produce a homemade chocolate roulade – this one has the added temptation of a strawberry cream filling.

Serves 6

ingredients

175 g (6 oz) plain chocolate, roughly chopped, plus extra for chocolate curls to decorate
6 large eggs, separated
175 g (6 oz) golden caster sugar
Cocoa powder, to dust
Single cream, to finish

for the filling

1 x 300 ml carton double cream
Finely grated zest and juice of 1 small orange
6 tbsp Bonne Maman Strawberry Conserve

method

Preheat the oven to 180°C (fan oven 160°C), gas mark 4. Line a 28 x 38 cm (11 x 15 inch) Swiss roll tin with non-stick baking parchment, making sure the top edge is about 2.5 cm (1 inch) above the level of the tin.

Put the chocolate in a small heatproof bowl with 150 ml (¼ pint) water and melt slowly over a pan of gently simmering water. Stir until smooth, then leave to cool slightly.

Whisk the egg yolks and caster sugar together using an electric whisk (mixer or hand-held) until very thick and pale. Add the cooled chocolate and stir until evenly blended. Whisk the egg whites until they form soft peaks.

Fold about one-third of the egg whites into the chocolate mixture using a large metal spoon. Fold in the remaining egg whites. Pour into the prepared tin and bake in the preheated oven for 20–25 minutes or until just firm. Put a wire rack over the tin and cover with a damp tea towel. Leave overnight.

To make the filling, whip the cream until it just holds its shape. In a separate bowl, stir the orange zest and 1 tablespoon of juice into the conserve.

Dust a large piece of non-stick baking parchment with icing sugar. Flip the roulade, cooked side down, onto the parchment and peel off the lining paper.

Spread the roulade with the whipped cream and then dot evenly with the conserve. Roll up the roulade, keeping it as tight as possible, and pull away the paper. Cover lightly with cling film and keep chilled until needed.

Decorate with chocolate curls and serve in slices with chilled single cream.

COOK'S TIP
* The roulade also has an optional chocolate coating that looks impressive but is very simple to do. Cut out a sheet of baking parchment the same diameter and length as the rolled roulade. Put the roulade in the freezer for 30 minutes. Brush the parchment all over with a thin layer of melted chocolate, about 100 g (3½ oz). Remove the roulade from the freezer and drape the paper over the roulade, melted chocolate side down. Press down evenly all over. Return to the freezer for 20 minutes, then gently peel away the paper and you will be left with a crisp chocolate covering. Keep in the fridge and dust lightly with cocoa powder before serving.

White Chocolate and Raspberry Tartlets

An irresistible mouthful of chocolate and fresh berries – perfect for enjoying on a quiet afternoon while immersing yourself in a can't-put-down book.

Makes 12 small tartlets

ingredients

125 g (4 oz) filo pastry
25 g (1 oz) butter, melted
8 tbsp Bonne Maman Raspberry
   Conserve
1 tbsp fresh orange or lemon
   juice
12 small raspberries
12 blueberries

for the mousse

50 g (2 oz) good-quality white
   chocolate, plus extra to
   decorate
1 x 150 ml carton double cream
1 sheet of leaf gelatine
1 small egg, separated
25 g (1 oz) caster sugar

to decorate

Fresh mint sprigs
Icing sugar

method

Preheat the oven to 190°C (fan oven 170°C), gas mark 5. Invert 6 small dariole moulds on a baking sheet.

Cut each sheet of filo pastry into about 6 rectangles and keep them covered with a damp tea towel while working. Using half the pastry, drape the rectangles in twisted layers over the moulds, brushing very lightly with melted butter between each one.

Bake in the preheated oven for 9–10 minutes until pale golden and crisp. Leave to cool for 10 minutes, then ease off the moulds. Repeat with the remaining pastry to make 12 tartlet cases.

To make the mousse, chop the chocolate into 50 ml (2 fl oz) of the cream in a heatproof bowl and melt slowly over a pan of gently simmering water.

Cut the leaf gelatine into small pieces, put in a bowl with 2 tablespoons water and leave to soak for 10 minutes. Pour the gelatine and water into the chocolate cream and stir gently until dissolved. Stir in the egg yolk.

In a clean bowl, whisk the egg white until it forms soft peaks, then gradually whisk in all the caster sugar until stiff. In a separate bowl, whisk the remaining cream until it just begins to hold its shape.

Put 1 teaspoon of conserve into the base of each tartlet case. Using a metal spoon, fold the egg white and whipped cream into the chocolate and spoon immediately on top of the conserve. Chill for at least 30 minutes to set.

Stir together the remaining conserve with the citrus juice and gently fold in the raspberries and blueberries. Just before serving, spoon the fruit onto the chocolate mousse, decorate with mint sprigs and a dusting of icing sugar.

COOK'S TIPS

❋ To prepare ahead, complete the filled filo tartlets and freeze. Stir the fruit into the conserve about 2 hours before needed and chill. Thaw the tartlets in the fridge for 20 minutes, top with fruit and serve.

❋ If you don't want to make the tartlets, spoon the conserve into small shot glasses, top with the mousse as above and chill to set.

❋ If you don't have dariole moulds to shape the tartlets, use scrunched up balls of kitchen foil.

Easter fun

Eastertide heralds the arrival of spring with
its fresh lively colours, pretty flowers and brightly
decorated eggs. As well as Easter egg hunts children
will love the fun of creating Easter decorations and
cards. Bonne Maman jars make ideal receptacles for
the odds and ends involved – appliqué flowers, mini
painted wooden eggs, ribbons, bows and little fluffy
chicks; all can be easily seen and stored.

Warm Berries and Cherries Sauce

Get all the sunny flavours of spring and summer with this simple fruit sauce. It's made in minutes and is so useful to have on hand in the fridge for an instant pudding.

Makes enough to fill 2 Victoria sponge cakes

ingredients

6 generous tbsp Bonne Maman
   Berries and Cherries Conserve
4 tbsp red grape juice
1 tsp arrowroot
125 g (4 oz) frozen raspberries
2 tbsp Grand Marnier or
   Cointreau liqueur

method

Put the conserve and grape juice in a small saucepan and warm through, stirring, until evenly blended.

Mix the arrowroot with 3 teaspoons cold water and stir into the pan. Bring to the boil, stirring, and bubble for 1–2 minutes until lightly thickened.

Remove the pan from the heat and stir in the frozen raspberries and liqueur. Serve warm or chilled.

COOK'S TIPS

* The sauce can be kept chilled in a jar in the fridge for up to 1 week or spoon into a freezer-proof bag and freeze. To use, thaw in the fridge and serve chilled or warm through for 1 minute before using.
* If you don't want to add the liqueur as suggested, use the same quantity of fresh orange juice.
* Serve the sauce warm over good-quality vanilla ice cream, spoon it onto a lemon tart or add a swirl to some whipped cream to sandwich together a sponge cake.
* The sauce also makes the most delicious trifle with layers of sponge cake, custard and cream.

Mandarin and Mango Tart

This makes an excellent Sunday lunch pudding served with crème fraîche or sliced into slim fingers for a coffee morning.

Serves 6–8

ingredients

1 x 375 g pack chilled shortcrust pastry
50 g (2 oz) self-raising flour, plus extra for dusting
1 cardamom pod, split
75 g (3 oz) unsalted butter
75 g (3 oz) light muscovado sugar
75 g (3 oz) ground hazelnuts
2 eggs, beaten
6 tbsp Bonne Maman Mandarin Marmalade
1 small, ripe mango, peeled, stoned and roughly chopped
Finely grated zest and juice of 1 lime

method

Preheat the oven to 180°C (fan oven 160°C), gas mark 4.

Roll out the pastry on a lightly floured surface. Line a shallow tranche tin, 35 x 12 x 2.5 cm (14 x 5 x 1 inch), with the pastry and chill until firm.

Line the pastry case with foil, gently easing the foil into the fluted edges and up over the top. Sprinkle a handful of dried beans or pulses into the foil and bake 'blind' in the preheated oven for 20 minutes or until the pastry is cooked but still pale. Leave to cool, then carefully ease the foil and beans or pulses off the pastry.

Split open the cardamom pod and scrape out the little black seeds into a mortar or strong bowl. Using the pestle or the end of a rolling pin, pound the seeds to a powder. In a medium bowl, beat together the butter, sugar and ground cardamom seeds until very light and creamy.

Mix together the flour and hazelnuts. Beat the eggs into the creamed butter mixture adding a spoonful of the dry ingredients with each addition. Fold in the remaining flour mixture.

Spread half the marmalade over the pastry, then spoon the hazelnut mixture on top and scatter with the mango pieces. Bake in the preheated oven for 30–35 minutes, or until the filling is golden brown and firm to the touch.

Warm the remaining marmalade in a small saucepan with the lime zest and juice. Bring to the boil and when it is bubbling, brush the hot glaze over the surface of the tart. Leave to cool before serving.

COOK'S TIPS

* To prepare ahead, bake the tart up to 1 day ahead of time but don't glaze. Cover lightly and keep in a cool place or wrap and freeze. To use, thaw overnight if necessary and warm through in a moderate oven for 10–12 minutes. Glaze as above.
* This tart works equally well with chopped dessert apples or pears scattered over the hazelnut sponge. Try a little chopped stem ginger too.
* Omit the cardamom and replace with a pinch of ground cinnamon.

Lemon and Wild Blueberry Swirl Cake

A fresh and fruity cake – perfect for a springtime afternoon tea. It's so easy to do, in under 10 minutes it's ready to bake!

Serves 8

ingredients

175 g (6 oz) butter, softened
175 g (6 oz) caster sugar, plus
   extra for sprinkling
3 free-range eggs
200 g (7 oz) self-raising flour
25 g (1 oz) ground almonds
Grated zest of 1 unwaxed lemon
4 tbsp Bonne Maman Wild
   Blueberry Conserve

method

Preheat the oven to 180°C (fan oven 160°C), gas mark 4. Line a 900 g (2 lb) loaf tin or a 20 cm (8 inch) round cake tin with non-stick baking parchment.

Place all the ingredients except the conserve into a mixing bowl and using a hand-held electric whisk blend the ingredients together until smooth. Alternatively, beat with a wooden spoon for 2 minutes.

Spoon into the prepared tin and level with the back of a spoon. Place the wild blueberry conserve into a paper piping bag and snip off the end. Pipe a swirl of the conserve on the top of the cake.

Bake on the centre shelf in the preheated oven for about 40–50 minutes until a skewer pushed into the centre comes out clean. Sprinkle with a little extra caster sugar. Cool in the tin for 10 minutes then turn out and leave to cool completely on a wire rack.

COOK'S TIPS

* The cooled cake will freeze for up to 1 month. To use, thaw overnight at room temperature.
* If you don't want to pipe the conserve onto the cake mixture, just drop it from the end of a teaspoon.

Cappuccino Caramel Torte

This makes a wonderful Easter treat, but is perfect for any occasion, and it freezes beautifully. Don't worry about making the chocolate shards, they're simple to do and don't need to be perfect for a great effect.

Serves 10–12

ingredients

225 g (8 oz) unsalted butter, softened
225 g (8 oz) light muscovado sugar
200 g (7 oz) self-raising flour
25 g (1 oz) ground almonds
1 tsp baking powder
4 large eggs
1 tbsp instant coffee

for the caramel cream

1 x 300 ml carton double cream
250 g (9 oz) Bonne Maman Confiture de Caramel

to decorate

Shards of white chocolate
Mini easter eggs

method

Line an 18 x 9.5 cm (7 x 4 inch) deep round cake tin with baking parchment. Preheat the oven to 180°C (fan oven 160°C), gas mark 4.

Put all the cake ingredients, except the coffee, in a large bowl and using an electric whisk (mixer or hand-held), beat together until very smooth and creamy. Dissolve the coffee in 1 tablespoon boiling water and blend in.

Spoon the mixture into the tin and bake for about 45–55 minutes or until golden and firm to touch. A skewer pushed into the centre should come out clean. Cover loosely with foil if it begins to darken before the cake is cooked. Cool in the tin for 30 minutes before turning out onto a wire rack.

Meanwhile, make the caramel cream. Whip the double cream until it just begins to thicken and hold its shape. The whisk will leave a trail when lifted.

Change to a balloon whisk (to avoid over whipping) and add 2 generous tablespoons of confiture de caramel. Whisk until the cream again holds its shape. Add a further 2 tablespoons of caramel and whisk again until the cream retains its shape. Continue until all the caramel has been incorporated into the cream and the cream forms soft peaks. Divide the cream between two bowls.

Cut the cake in half, then split each half again to give four equal rounds. Put the round, which was the top of the cake, cut side up on a serving board or plate. Take one bowl of caramel cream and spread about a third over the cake, right to the edge. Top with a second round and repeat until all the cream is used. Finish with the round that was the base of the cooked cake, cooked side up, as this is the flattest. Press down lightly.

Spread the remaining bowl of cream over the top and sides of the cake. Decorate with shards of white chocolate and mini Easter eggs.

COOK'S TIP

* To make the chocolate shards, melt 200 g (7 oz) good-quality white chocolate over a pan of gently simmering water. On a clean baking sheet, spread the chocolate into a round about the thickness of a pound coin and chill for 1 hour. With a large, sharp knife, cut wafer thin slices off the round, starting at one edge of the chocolate. As you make the shards pop them into a container and into the fridge or freezer to keep firm.

Glazed Apricot Rice Pudding

A fruity rice pudding with a crunchy sugar topping – a great alternative to crème brûlée at the end of a fresh spring supper.

Serves 2

ingredients

750 ml (1¼ pints) whole milk
50 g (2 oz) butter
75 g (3 oz) caster sugar
100 g (3½ oz) pudding rice
3 heaped tbsp Bonne Maman
  Apricot Compote, plus extra
  to serve

method

Heat the milk in a saucepan until just below boiling point. Turn off the heat.

Meanwhile, melt the butter in a separate saucepan, but don't allow it to brown. Stir in 50 g (2 oz) of the sugar and heat until it has dissolved. Add the rice and cook for 1 minute until coated and glossy.

Gradually add ladlefuls of warm milk, stirring continuously so the rice doesn't stick to the pan. Continue to add the milk gradually, stirring continuously, until you have a thick, glossy pudding and the rice is cooked through – you may not need all of the milk. Remove from the heat and stir in the compote until just combined.

Preheat the grill to high. Divide the mixture between 2 heatproof serving bowls and leave to stand for 1 minute. Sprinkle over the remaining sugar and put under the grill for 2–3 minutes until it browns and bubbles. This can be done with a chef's blowtorch instead, if you like. Serve with an extra dollop of the compote.

COOK'S TIPS

* For a touch of spice, add a large pinch of ground cinnamon or a cinnamon stick to the cooking rice.
* When fresh raspberries are in season put 3 or 4 in the base of each dish before spooning over the rice mixture.

Rhubarb and Pear Crumble

A very different and simple idea to serve at a weekend brunch. Bake the crumble in something like a ceramic pie or soufflé dish to take to the table.

Serves 6

ingredients

600 g (1 lb 6 oz) ripe but firm
   pears, cored and roughly
   chopped
1 x 600 g jar Bonne Maman
   Rhubarb Compote
50 g (2 oz) plain flour
A large pinch of ground ginger
75 g (3 oz) golden caster sugar
100 g (3½ oz) chilled, unsalted
   butter, cubed
200 g (7 oz) natural, no-added
   sugar muesli
Greek yogurt, to finish

method

Preheat the oven to 190°C (fan oven 170°C), gas mark 5.

Stir the chopped pear into the rhubarb compote and spoon into a small but deep, non-metallic ovenproof dish.

Rub together the flour, spice, sugar and butter until the mixture looks like rough crumbs. Stir in the muesli and spoon over the top of the fruit.

Bake in the preheated oven for 30 minutes, or until the topping is golden and crisp. Serve hot with Greek yogurt.

COOK'S TIPS

* Up to 1 day ahead, make the fruit mixture and spoon into the dish. Cover with cling film and chill. Make the crumble mixture and store in the fridge in a polythene bag. To use, assemble the crumble and bake as above.
* Stir a little grated orange zest and orange juice into the rhubarb mixture or sprinkle a few chopped nuts onto the crumble mixture before baking.

Pretty flavoured sugars for your baking.

Strawberry Soufflés

Soufflés can be tricky to get right, but this easy version is a cinch and a great dessert to impress. Enjoy the taste of summer early in the year in one little dish!

Serves 4

ingredients

1 tbsp butter

4 large free-range egg whites

125 g (4 oz) caster sugar

4 tbsp Bonne Maman Strawberry
Conserve

1 tbsp icing sugar, to dust

method

Preheat the oven to 200°C (fan oven 180°C), gas mark 6. Lightly grease 4 individual deep ramekin dishes with the butter. Put the dishes into a medium roasting tin.

Whisk the egg whites in a clean, dry bowl until stiff, then whisk in the sugar, a spoonful at a time, until it is thick and glossy. Fold in the conserve, then spoon the soufflé mixture into the prepared ramekin dishes.

Bake on a centre shelf in the preheated oven for 12–15 minutes.

Lightly dust with the icing sugar and serve immediately.

COOK'S TIPS

* For an equally gorgeous soufflé, try Bonne Maman Berries and Cherries, Blackcurrant or Raspberry Conserve.

* Put a small scoop of solid ice cream in the base of each ramekin before adding the meringue for a Baked Alaska-type pudding.

été
summer

Savoury Picnic Tartlets

These are perfect for a picnic with some crunchy salad or served warm as a starter for a summer's evening supper.

Serves 6

ingredients

3 large Spanish onions, thinly sliced
3 fat garlic cloves, thinly sliced
3 tbsp olive oil
50 g (2 oz) butter
A handful of fresh rosemary sprigs
8 tbsp Bonne Maman Peach Conserve
100 ml (3½ fl oz) dry white wine
1 x 375 g chilled, ready-rolled puff pastry
1 large egg, beaten
3 tbsp mascarpone cheese
25 g (1 oz) Roquefort or any soft, blue-veined cheese
6 thick slices goats' cheese
Freshly ground black pepper

method

Preheat the oven to 220°C (fan oven 200°C), gas mark 7.

Tip the onions and garlic into a large sauté pan with the olive oil, butter and about 1 tablespoon of rosemary leaves taken from the handful of sprigs. Cook, stirring, over a low heat until the onions are very soft and a deep, golden brown. This will take a good 15–20 minutes.

Add the peach conserve and wine and bring to the boil. Bubble gently, stirring, until the onions are sticky and glazed with most of the liquid evaporated. Leave to cool.

Unroll the puff pastry sheet and stamp out 6 x 12 cm (5 inch) rounds. Place on a baking sheet and, with a sharp knife, score an inner circle about 1 cm (½ inch) in from the edge. Brush the pastry lightly with some of the egg and bake in the preheated oven for 8 minutes or until pale golden brown.

Spoon the caramelised onions into the centre of each tartlet case. Beat together the mascarpone, remaining egg and the blue cheese in a separate bowl. Dip the goats' cheese slices into the mixture to coat lightly, then sit them on top of the onions. Season with pepper and a few extra rosemary leaves, then bake for a further 8–10 minutes or until the cheese is pale golden and beginning to melt.

COOK'S TIPS
* There are many different types of goats' cheese available. Opt for a long log and cut into slices with a hot knife.
* For a party nibble, bake ready-made vol-au-vent cases and fill with the soft onion mixture and a spoonful of soft goats' cheese. Warm through in a hot oven for 10 minutes.

Chicken Liver and Wild Mushroom Pâté

No shop-bought pâté will ever be as velvety and rich in flavour as this homemade recipe. The rewards are well worth the effort and it freezes beautifully.

Serves 6–8

ingredients

25 g (1 oz) dried porcini
  mushrooms
150 g (5 oz) butter, softened
1 large Spanish onion, finely
  chopped
4 sprigs of fresh rosemary
2 fat garlic cloves, crushed
225 g (8 oz) chicken livers,
  trimmed and soaked in milk for
  30 minutes
2 smoked streaky bacon
  rashers, roughly chopped
7 tbsp Bonne Maman Apricot
  Conserve
2 tbsp brandy
1½ sheets of leaf gelatine
1 tsp coarsely ground black
  peppercorns

method

Soak the porcini mushrooms in 200 ml (7 fl oz) water for 30 minutes. Drain and reserve the soaking liquid.

Melt 25 g (1 oz) of the butter in a large frying pan and fry the onion with half the rosemary, the soaked mushrooms and the garlic until very soft and golden brown – this will take a good 10 minutes. Remove from the pan with a slotted spoon and set aside. Discard the rosemary sprigs.

Drain the livers. Add a further 25 g (1 oz) of the butter to the pan, increase the heat and fry the livers briskly with the bacon until deep golden on the outside and still pink in the centre – this should take no longer than 3–4 minutes. Stir in 1 tablespoon of the conserve, the brandy and the onion mixture. Remove the pan from the heat and leave to cool.

Liquidise the liver mixture with the remaining butter to a smooth paste and spoon into an earthenware dish. Cover with cling film and chill for 30 minutes.

Meanwhile, put the reserved mushroom liquid into a small saucepan. Cut the gelatine into small pieces and drop into the pan. Leave to soak for 10 minutes. Warm over a low heat until the gelatine dissolves, then stir in the remaining conserve.

Spoon this mixture over the chilled pâté and top with the remaining rosemary sprigs and peppercorns. Chill for a further 1 hour.

COOK'S TIPS
* The pâté will keep in the fridge for up to 1 week.
* It can be made ahead of time and frozen. Add the jelly up to 1 week before needed.
* This pâté is particularly delicious with thin slices of toasted brioche.
* For a special occasion, take the time to push the liquidised liver mixture through a mesh sieve using a rubber spatula. It is time-consuming and adds to the washing up but produces a wonderful velvety rich texture.

Blackened Tuna Steaks with Sweet Chilli Glaze

With these steaks marinating in the fridge, supper can be ready in minutes: perfect to come home to after a busy summer's day. This is a fast, fresh and easy way to cook tuna.

Serves 4

ingredients

4 responsibly sourced, fresh
   tuna steaks, weighing about
   150 g (5 oz) each
Sesame seeds, for sprinkling

for the marinade

1 shallot, finely chopped
3 garlic cloves, sliced
3 tbsp vegetable oil
1 tsp ground turmeric
A large pinch of dried chilli
   flakes
2.5 cm (1 inch) piece of
   fresh ginger, peeled and
   finely grated
4 tbsp Bonne Maman Mandarin
   Marmalade
3 tbsp ketjap manis or sweet
   soy sauce
1 tbsp Thai fish sauce

to finish

Cooked rice noodles
Stir-fried green vegetables
Lime wedges

method

Fry the shallot and garlic in the oil until soft and golden brown. Stir in the turmeric, chilli flakes and ginger and cook for a further minute before removing from the heat and adding the remaining marinade ingredients. Stir well and leave to cool.

Put the tuna into a shallow, non-metallic dish and spoon over the marinade. Cover and leave to marinate in the fridge overnight.

Lift the tuna from the marinade, brushing off any excess. Put the marinade in a small saucepan and bring to the boil. Bubble for 2–3 minutes and set aside.

Cook the tuna on a preheated griddle or frying pan over a high heat for 2–3 minutes on each side until deep golden and glazed. Sprinkle the steaks with sesame seeds and serve with rice noodles, some stir-fried green vegetables, wedges of lime and the hot marinade.

COOK'S TIPS

∗ The tuna can be left in the marinade for up to 3 days. Alternatively, freeze the tuna steaks in the marinade.

∗ The marinade can also be used with other ingredients for the barbecue: try jumbo prawns, chicken skewers and Portobello mushrooms.

Warm Fig, Blue Cheese and Hazelnut Salad

Such a simple summer salad but it looks and tastes wonderful – and is so easy to do. Have all the ingredients ready ahead of time and the salad can be assembled in minutes.

Serves 6

ingredients

6 plump, ripe but firm, fresh figs
250 g (9 oz) blue cheese, such
    as Roquefort, Saint Agur or
    Bleu d'Auvergne
125 g (4 oz) soft salad leaves
25 g (1 oz) hazelnuts, skinned,
    toasted and roughly chopped
Walnut bread, to serve

for the dressing

2 tbsp Bonne Maman
    Blackcurrant Conserve
3 tbsp extra virgin olive oil
1 tbsp hazelnut oil
1 tbsp sherry or white wine
    vinegar

method

Halve the figs from tip to base. Cover and keep chilled. Crumble the cheese, cover and keep chilled.

Put all the dressing ingredients in a jar and shake until thoroughly combined. Keep in the fridge until needed.

Divide the crumbled cheese between 6 individual serving plates a couple of hours before serving and pile a handful of salad leaves in the centre. Cover lightly with cling film and keep chilled.

When ready to serve, brush the cut side of the figs with a little of the dressing. Heat a small frying pan over a high heat and fry the figs, cut side down, for 1–2 minutes or until just beginning to turn golden.

Arrange 2 fig halves on each plate of salad and cheese, drizzle over a little dressing and some of the chopped hazelnuts and serve immediately with thin slices of walnut bread.

COOK'S TIPS
* The dressing benefits from being made up to 3 days ahead and can be kept in the fridge. Up to 1 day ahead, crumble the cheese. About 2 hours before serving, prepare the salad as above. Remove the dressing from the fridge to come to room temperature before serving.
* For the prettiest salad, include some red leaves such as wild rocket with chard or a mixed baby leaf salad.
* The dressing is also wonderful served with a salad of wafer-thin smoked duck slices.

Roasted Pork Fillet with Tangled Peppers

This fruity marinade adds an elegance to the pork fillet and served with the tangle of braised peppers and a cool watercress salad makes it a perfect meal for entertaining.

Serves 3–4

ingredients

2.5 cm (1 inch) piece of fresh
   ginger, peeled and grated
1 garlic clove, crushed
Juice of 1 lime
1 tbsp olive oil
1 tbsp Bonne Maman Raspberry
   Conserve
1 large tenderloin of pork,
   weighing about 450 g (1 lb)
Watercress or rocket, to serve

for the peppers

2 tbsp olive oil
6 red peppers, deseeded and
   finely sliced
1 large Spanish onion, finely
   sliced
2 garlic cloves, finely sliced
2 tbsp chopped fresh basil
Salt and freshly ground black
   pepper

method

Blend together the ginger, garlic, lime juice, olive oil and conserve in a large shallow bowl.

Lightly score the pork fillet on both sides and add it to the bowl. Coat the meat completely with the marinade, cover and leave to marinate in the fridge for at least 2 hours or up to 24 hours.

Preheat the oven to 240°C (fan oven 220°C), gas mark 9.

Put a rack in a roasting tin and add about 2.5 cm (1 inch) water to the tin. Place the pork fillet on the rack, baste with some of the marinade and roast in the preheated oven for 20–30 minutes, turning the fillet over after about 15 minutes and basting with any remaining marinade.

Meanwhile, make the tangled peppers. Heat the olive oil in a wide pan until hot. Add the peppers and onions and cook, stirring constantly, for 5 minutes or so until beginning to soften. Add the garlic and stir well.

Reduce the heat and allow to cook gently for another 15–20 minutes, stirring occasionally, until completely softened. Stir in the basil, season to taste and set aside until needed.

Remove the pork from the oven and allow it to rest for 10 minutes. Reheat the peppers if necessary, then slice the pork thinly and serve with the tangled peppers and a watercress or rocket salad.

COOK'S TIPS
* Use the same marinade for pork chops before grilling.
* Make the tangled peppers to serve with hot, cooked gammon and stir in
   1 tablespoon of Bonne Maman Apricot Conserve with a squeeze of lemon.

Picnic perfect

On a beautiful summer's day what could be more enjoyable than to set out for a picnic, away from the crowds under the shade of a large tree, with a hamper of delicious food. There's something very special about eating outside and why not add charm to the occasion by serving up some of the food in Bonne Maman jars?

From individual servings of fresh chilled soups, to croutons, toasted nuts and delicious dressings for salads; even salt and pepper look attractive in the pretty red-and-white topped mini pots.

Sizzling Chilli and Peach Chicken

This unusual flavour combination makes for a lovely summer meal and will definitely get your taste buds tingling.

Serves 4

ingredients

50 g (2 oz) palm sugar or dark muscovado sugar

1 tsp ground turmeric

1 red chilli, deseeded and finely shredded

5 cm (2 inch) piece of fresh ginger, peeled and finely grated

3 tbsp fish sauce

Juice of 2 limes

4 tbsp Bonne Maman Peach Conserve

8 boned chicken thighs, skin on

2 tbsp light oil, such as rapeseed

3 fat garlic cloves, sliced

to finish

Shredded spring onion

Fresh mint

Chopped salted peanuts

1 lime, quartered

method

Put the sugar, turmeric and 3 tablespoons water in a small saucepan and heat slowly, stirring, for 2–3 minutes until the sugar has dissolved.

Add the chilli, ginger, fish sauce, lime juice and conserve. Increase the heat and bubble for 1–2 minutes until a deep, golden caramel brown. Remove from the heat.

Cut the chicken into large, bite-sized pieces. Heat the oil in a large wok or frying pan and fry the chicken with the garlic for 3–4 minutes, until golden brown and crisp.

Pour in half the chilli peach caramel and let it bubble up and sizzle for 2–3 minutes.

Sprinkle with spring onions, mint and peanuts, squeeze over a little lime and serve immediately. Offer the remaining chilli peach caramel separately.

COOK'S TIPS

* The chicken is also delicious served cold with salad.
* Cut the hot chicken into fine shreds and serve in wrap breads with soured cream and soft salad leaves.
* Try the recipe with 450 g (1 lb) raw king prawns.

Slow-braised Lamb with Cherries and Saffron

This is a useful recipe to have on hand at any time of year. It's quick to assemble, looks after itself in the oven and can be made ahead and frozen.

Serves 6–8

ingredients

700 g (1½ lb) boned shoulder of lamb, cut into large pieces
1 tsp ground cumin
1 tsp dried thyme
3 garlic cloves, crushed
Pared zest and juice of 2 large oranges
50 g (2 oz) small dried apricots
1 tsp saffron strands
150 ml (¼ pint) medium sherry
1 tbsp sherry or white wine vinegar
1 tbsp olive oil, plus extra for frying
2 tbsp flour
4 tbsp Bonne Maman Cherry Compote
2 tbsp honey
300 ml (½ pint) chicken or vegetable stock
Salt and freshly ground black pepper

to finish

Cooked pilaf rice
Freshly chopped parsley

method

Put the lamb in a large glass bowl with the cumin, thyme, garlic, orange zest and juice, apricots, saffron, sherry, vinegar and the 1 tablespoon of olive oil. Cover and leave to marinate in the fridge overnight.

Preheat the oven to 170°C (fan oven 150°C), gas mark 3.

Lift the lamb from the marinade and pat dry. Heat a good drizzle of olive oil in a medium-sized lidded casserole dish, and brown the lamb a few pieces at a time. Getting a good colour on the meat ensures that the finished cooking juices will be rich and dark, so it's worth taking the time at this stage.

Return all the meat to the pan and stir in the flour. Pour in the marinade mixture along with the compote, honey and stock. Bring to the boil, cover tightly and cook in the preheated oven for 1½ –2 hours or until the meat is very tender. Adjust the seasoning and serve with a light pilaf and sprinkled with chopped parsley.

COOK'S TIPS

* The lamb can be cooked up to 3 days ahead of time and kept in the fridge. Reheat gently on the hob. Alternatively, freeze until needed.
* It's best to buy a boned shoulder of lamb and cut into large pieces at home. Avoid ready-diced lamb as it is invariably cut too small and shrinks even further when cooked.
* You could also serve the lamb with a simple salad and crusty bread.

Fresh Peach and Parma Ham Salad

Fresh peaches are one of the great tastes of summer. Try them with salty Parma ham, peppery leaves and a fruity dressing.

Serves 6

ingredients

6 just-ripe peaches, halved, stoned and thickly sliced
12 thin slices Parma ham
About 125 g (4 oz) wild rocket or baby leaf watercress

for the dressing

2 tbsp white wine or sherry vinegar
3 tbsp extra virgin olive oil
1 tbsp Bonne Maman Peach Conserve
1 tsp finely chopped red chilli

method

First make the dressing by putting all the ingredients in a jar and giving them a good shake until well blended.

Put the peach slices in a non-metallic bowl and pour over the dressing. Cover and leave to marinate in the fridge for 2–3 hours.

When ready to serve, simply curl 2 slices of ham per person on individual serving plates. Toss the leaves with the peaches and dressing in a large bowl, then divide between the serving plates. Serve immediately.

COOK'S TIPS

* The dressing can be made up to 1 week ahead and kept in the fridge. Allow 15 minutes at room temperature before using.
* The dressing is equally good with slices of mixed melon or pieces of fresh mango or papaya.

Summer Greens with Bitter Orange Butter Dressing

This fresh buttery dressing is delicious served over any freshly steamed summer greens such as French beans, runner beans, peas or long-stemmed, purple sprouting broccoli.

Serves 6

ingredients

3 small egg yolks

200 g (7 oz) unsalted butter, melted and hot

1 tbsp Bonne Maman Bitter Orange Marmalade

2 generous tbsp crème fraîche

1 tbsp chopped flat-leaf parsley, chives or chervil

450 g (1 lb) runner beans

225 g (8 oz) podded fresh peas

method

Put the egg yolks in a heatproof bowl and sit it over a pan of very gently simmering water. With a wooden spoon, beat the yolks for 1–2 minutes over the heat before gradually adding the hot melted butter, a drizzle at a time. Beat well between each addition and the egg yolks should gradually begin to thicken and turn creamy.

Add the marmalade and stir until melted and combined, then fold in the crème fraîche and chopped herbs. Remove the pan from the heat but leave the bowl on top of the warm water. Cover with cling film and stir occasionally. This will keep the dressing warm for up to 30 minutes.

Drop the runner beans into a large saucepan of boiling, salted water. Return to the boil and cook for 5 minutes. Add the peas and continue to cook for a further 2–3 minutes until both are tender. Drain well and serve with the bitter orange dressing.

COOK'S TIPS

* The dressing can be made up to 30 minutes ahead but no longer or it may start to separate.
* Serve the warm dressing with grilled salmon steaks or steamed new carrots. It's also delicious as a dip for fresh asparagus.

Walnut and Mint Pesto

Although this sauce is called a pesto it does not include any cheese or basil. It's delicious tossed through hot, pappardelle pasta with added olives and crumbled feta cheese, but equally good on top of oven-baked fish fillets or grilled chicken breasts.

Serves 4–6

ingredients

A large bunch of fresh parsley
A handful of fresh mint leaves
1 garlic clove
Finely grated zest of 2 lemons
50 g (2 oz) toasted walnuts
4 tbsp walnut oil
2 tbsp good-quality olive oil, plus extra for covering the pesto
2 tbsp Bonne Maman Apricot Compote
1 small red chilli, deseeded and finely chopped (optional)

method

Strip the leaves from the parsley and mint and whizz in a food processor or blender with the garlic until roughly chopped.

Add the lemon zest and walnuts and whizz again for a few seconds. Finally, add the oils, compote and chilli, if using. Process to a rough paste.

Spoon the paste into a clean jar. Pour on a little extra olive oil to cover the surface of the pesto and keep in the fridge until needed.

COOK'S TIPS

* The pesto will keep in the fridge for up to 1 week.
* It's delicious when spread under the skin of chicken fillets before roasting or added to hot grilled pork chops or mackerel.
* For a vegetarian supper, grill some large Portobello mushrooms until golden and tender. Serve with a dollop of soured cream and the Walnut and Mint Pesto.

Homemade bouquet garni stored and ready for cooking.

Avocado, Prawn and Cabbage Salad

This simple salad takes minimum effort for maximum wow factor! It's perfect for any summer picnic or party buffet.

Serves 6

ingredients

6 fat garlic cloves, thinly sliced
2 tbsp vegetable oil
350 g (12 oz) raw shelled
    prawns
25 g (1 oz) roasted cashew nuts,
    finely chopped
1 ripe avocado
125 g (4 oz) white cabbage,
    finely shredded
1 small green mango, peeled,
    stoned and shredded
A small handful of fresh mint
    and coriander leaves, roughly
    chopped
6 spring onions, shredded

for the dressing

½ red chilli, deseeded and finely
    chopped
1 tbsp rice wine vinegar
2 generous tbsp Bonne Maman
    Apricot Conserve
Juice of 2 limes
1 tbsp fish sauce
2 tbsp vegetable oil

method

Put all the dressing ingredients in a jar and shake together.

Fry the garlic in the oil in a heavy-based saucepan over a medium heat until golden and crispy. Remove from the oil with a slotted spoon and set aside.

In the same oil, stir-fry the prawns with the roasted cashew nuts for about 2–3 minutes until the prawns are just pink. Add to the garlic, spoon over 2 tablespoons of the dressing and set aside to cool.

When ready to serve, peel, stone and dice the avocado, and toss together with the cabbage, mango, herbs, spring onions and prawn mixture. Serve immediately, handing round the remaining dressing in a separate bowl.

COOK'S TIPS

* Make the dressing up to 1 week ahead and keep in a jar in the fridge. Cook the prawn mixture the day before needed. Keep chilled and toss everything together just before serving.
* This dressing is also delicious spooned over pan-fried chicken fillets and served with basmati rice.

Strawberry Ripple Ice Cream

This must be one of the simplest homemade ice cream recipes, ever! It has the dreamiest creamy texture, is bursting with flavour, needs no churning and, by using yogurt it is lower in fat than many other more traditional recipes.

Serves 4–6

ingredients

1 x 300 ml carton double cream

300 ml (½ pint) full-fat Greek yogurt

275 g (10 oz) Bonne Maman Strawberry Conserve

2 tbsp liqueur, such as Crème de Cassis

3–4 sugared rose petals, crushed

4–6 waffle cones, to finish

method

Whip the cream in a large bowl until it just begins to hold its shape. Fold in the yogurt and 200 g (7 oz) of the conserve.

Spoon half the mixture into a freezer-proof container that is about 5 cm (2 inches) deep.

Stir the liqueur into the remaining conserve in a separate bowl and drizzle over the top of the cream mixture in the container.

Spoon over the remaining cream mixture and freeze for at least 3 hours (depending on depth of container). Serve in cones or scoops with crushed, sugared rose petals sprinkled on top.

COOK'S TIPS

* The ice cream should be made one day and eaten the next. As it is a no-churn recipe, the longer it remains in the freezer the more ice crystals grow and it loses its creamy texture.

* Soften the ice cream in the fridge for about 30 minutes before using.

* For extra crunch, sprinkle 25 g (1 oz) crushed Bonne Maman Galettes over the strawberry conserve before freezing.

Pear and Fig Baklava

This is based on the traditional Middle Eastern pudding that layers wafer-thin sheets of filo pastry with chopped nuts and a sweet syrup. Baklava is expensive to buy, and you may think that it's difficult to make at home but this recipe is not challenging and quite delicious with the addition of fig and fresh pear.

Makes about 16

ingredients

10 tbsp Bonne Maman Fig Conserve

Finely grated zest of 2 small lemons

A large pinch of ground cinnamon

25 g (1 oz) toasted sesame seeds

½ tsp coarse ground black peppercorns (optional)

75 g (3 oz) toasted blanched almonds, finely chopped

50 g (2 oz) shelled pistachio nuts, finely chopped

4 tbsp golden caster sugar

75 g (3 oz) butter, melted

1 x 270 g pack filo pastry (12 sheets)

225 g (8 oz) ripe pears, peeled, cored and thinly sliced

method

Preheat the oven to 200°C (fan oven 180°C), gas mark 6.

Put the conserve in a medium saucepan with 150 ml (¼ pint) water and half the lemon zest. Bring to the boil, stirring, and bubble gently for 5–7 minutes until it forms a lightly thickened and sticky syrup. Set aside to cool.

In a pestle and mortar or in a strong bowl with the end of a rolling pin, pound the cinnamon, sesame seeds and peppercorns, if using, together to make a coarse powder. Stir in the nuts, sugar and remaining lemon zest.

Brush a 24 cm (9½ inch) square, 5 cm (2 inch) deep cake tin lightly with a little of the melted butter. Layer 6 sheets of the pastry over the bottom of the tin, brushing each one lightly with butter. Trim to fit.

Sprinkle half the nut mixture over the pastry and top with the sliced pears. Sprinkle over the remaining nut mixture and finish with a further 6 layers of filo, brushing lightly between each sheet with butter as before.

Bake in the preheated oven for 25–30 minutes or until golden brown. With a sharp knife, cut through the hot pastry to make 16 squares. Spoon over the cold conserve syrup and leave to cool.

COOK'S TIPS

* The cooked baklava will keep for 2–3 days in an airtight tin.
* Serve warm with crème fraîche as a pudding or cold with coffee.
* When working with filo pastry, unfold the sheets onto a clean tea towel, then cover with a second lightly damp towel to prevent the pastry from drying out while you work.
* The peppercorns are optional in this recipe, but they do give the baklava a mild spiciness that offsets the sweetness of the syrup.

Berry Profiteroles

Choux pastry sounds daunting but is probably one of the simplest pastries to make and the results are stunning and light.

Makes 12

ingredients

60 g (2½ oz) strong plain flour
1 tsp golden caster sugar
50 g (2 oz) butter
2 large eggs, beaten
1 x 250 g tub mascarpone
  cheese
175 ml (6 fl oz) ready-made,
  chilled Crème Anglaise or
  Vanilla Custard
4 generous tbsp Bonne Maman
  Raspberry Conserve
1 x 100 g punnet fresh
  raspberries
1 x 100 g punnet fresh
  strawberries, hulled and sliced
Icing sugar, to dust

method

Preheat the oven to 200°C (fan oven 180°C), gas mark 6. Line 1 or 2 baking sheets with non-stick baking parchment.

Sift the flour onto a plate and add the sugar.

Put the butter in a small saucepan with 150 ml (¼ pint) cold water. Heat gently until the butter has melted, then bring to the boil. When the liquid is bubbling furiously remove the pan from the heat and pour in all the flour off the plate. Beat with a wooden spoon until the flour has been blended into the liquid. Gradually beat in the eggs until the mixture is a thick, smooth and glossy paste.

Drop dessertspoonfuls of choux paste onto the baking sheet/s, leaving about 2.5 cm (1 inch) between each one.

Bake the choux buns in the preheated oven for 15 minutes, then increase the oven temperature to 220°C (fan oven 200°C), gas mark 7 and continue to cook for a further 10–15 minutes or until golden and crisp on top.

Remove from the oven and make a slit in the side of each bun to allow the steam to escape. Put on a wire rack to cool completely.

Meanwhile, put the mascarpone in a bowl and gradually beat in the custard until smooth.

When ready to serve, put 1 teaspoon of conserve in the base of each bun, fill with the mascarpone custard and top with a mixture of fruits. Replace the top and dust with icing sugar to serve. Serve straight away.

COOK'S TIPS

* The choux buns can be made the day before and stored in an airtight container. When ready to use, warm in a low oven for 5 minutes. Cool and fill as above.
* Strong plain flour is used here as the extra gluten gives the finished buns a lighter, crispier texture.
* For a large party, make bite-sized buns by dropping just a teaspoon of mixture on the baking sheets and cook for 10 minutes at the lower temperature and then a further 10 minutes to brown.

Apricot Meringue Roulade

Crisp on the outside and gooey in the middle with a rich, creamy fruity filling – this is the perfect summer dessert.

Serves 6

ingredients

5 large free-range egg whites
275 g (10 oz) caster sugar, plus
   extra for rolling
50 g (2 oz) flaked almonds
Icing sugar, to dust

for the filling

1 x 300 ml carton double cream
4–5 tbsp Bonne Maman Apricot
   Compote

method

Preheat the oven to 220°C (fan oven 200°C), gas mark 7. Line a large baking sheet with non-stick baking parchment.

Place the egg whites in a grease-free, clean bowl and using a hand-held electric whisk, beat to stiff peaks.

Add the sugar very slowly with the electric whisk running at full speed until the meringue is stiff and shiny. This will take a good 5 minutes. Spread the meringue mixture onto the prepared baking sheet and level out. Sprinkle with the flaked almonds.

Bake in the centre of the preheated oven for 10 minutes. Reduce the temperature to 170°C (fan oven 150°C), gas mark 3 for about 15 minutes until firm on top but still soft and mallowy beneath.

Remove the meringue from the sheet and allow to cool. Turn out onto a clean sugared tea towel and remove the parchment paper.

To make the filling, whip the cream to soft peaks and spread onto the meringue. Lightly spread over the compote and roll up along the longest edge using the tea towel to form the roulade. Chill, then serve dusted with icing sugar.

COOK'S TIP

* For a lower-fat alternative, whip a 150 ml carton double cream until it just holds its shape, then fold in 150 ml (¼ pint) low-fat Greek yogurt and continue as above.

An original way to serve a refreshing summer punch.

Summer Brioche

A pudding that has the same delicious texture as traditional summer pudding but with none of the hassle of lining the bowl and the worry of turning it out! This is a great way to use up a glut of soft, summer fruit.

Serves 6

ingredients

6 tbsp Bonne Maman Black
  Cherry Conserve
350 ml (12 fl oz) chilled
  pomegranate and raspberry
  or pomegranate and blueberry
  juice
450 g (1 lb) raspberries
225 g (8 oz) small strawberries,
  hulled
Caster sugar, to taste
225 g (8 oz) brioche bread, cut
  into large bite-sized pieces
Crème fraîche, to serve

method

Put the conserve and juice in a small saucepan and heat together gently until the conserve has melted. Bring to the boil and bubble for 2–3 minutes until thick and syrupy.

Meanwhile, put the fruit in a large bowl and pour over the warm liquid. Sweeten to taste.

Layer the fruit and brioche in a glass serving bowl and pour over any remaining juice. Put a small plate on top, press down and add a weight. Chill overnight.

Serve the pudding in generous spoonfuls, straight from the fridge with crème fraîche.

COOK'S TIPS

✳ Make the pudding 1 day ahead and keep it chilled in the fridge.
✳ Any chilled juice can be used but make sure it is dark in colour as the brioche needs to soak it up to blend in with the fruit.
✳ The pudding can also be made in individual glasses or dishes but will be fiddlier to weigh down.

Tropical Fruits with Chilli Lime Syrup

This colourful fruit salad is the ideal pudding to serve after a rich, spicy main course; light and fresh with the fragrance of strawberries and the tang of lime.

Serves 6

ingredients

1 mango
12 lychees
1 papaya
½ Galia melon
2 bananas
½ pineapple

for the syrup

75 g (3 oz) golden caster sugar
Finely grated zest and juice of
   1 lime
4 tbsp Bonne Maman Strawberry
   and Wild Strawberry Conserve
½ red chilli, deseeded

method

Put all the syrup ingredients in a small saucepan with 300 ml (½ pint) cold water. Heat gently until the conserve has melted, then bring to the boil and bubble for 10 minutes until syrupy. Leave to cool.

Peel and stone the mango, cut into thick shreds and put in a large serving bowl. Peel and stone the lychees. Peel and deseed the papaya and melon and cut into similar-sized pieces. Add these to the bowl. Peel and slice the bananas and pineapple.

Stir all the fruit together and strain over the cooled syrup. Cover and chill for 3–4 hours before serving.

COOK'S TIPS

* Make the salad syrup up to 3 days ahead. Strain and keep chilled. Prepare the fruit up to 3–4 hours ahead and pour over the syrup. Keep chilled until needed.
* Any mixture of fruit can be used with this tangy syrup, just keep the quantity roughly the same.
* The chilli can be omitted but adds a gentle heat to the syrup that goes well with the sweetness of the strawberry and the sharpness of the lime.
* Drained, tinned lychees can be used here if fresh are not available.

Berries and Cherries Syllabub

This is a deliciously creamy concoction with a fruit and alcohol kick. Vary the liqueur used depending on your taste.

Serves 6

ingredients

125 g (4 oz) Bonne Maman
  Berries and Cherries Conserve
150 ml (¼ pint) medium white
  wine – Chardonnay is good
150 g (5 oz) caster sugar
1 tbsp Grand Marnier
2 tbsp Cassis
1 x 600 ml carton double cream
Bonne Maman Galettes, to serve

method

Place the conserve, wine, sugar, Grand Marnier and Cassis in a saucepan, stir to mix and leave over a very gentle heat for about 20 minutes or until the sugar has dissolved. Remove and allow to cool for about 30 minutes.

Add the cream to the conserve and wine mixture. Using a hand-held electric whisk, whisk until the mixture stands in soft peaks – this will take slightly longer than whisking cream due to the extra liquid. Take care not to over-whip as the mixture may separate.

Pipe or spoon into tall glasses and place in the refrigerator for 30 minutes to set. Serve with Bonne Maman Galettes.

COOK'S TIPS

* Add the cream to just half the conserve and wine mixture and continue as above. Divide the remaining conserve and wine mixture between the serving glasses and top with the syllabub to get a layered look.
* Try blending different Bonne Maman conserves and liqueurs for totally different puddings. Use Black Cherry Conserve with Cassis or Kirsch, Raspberry Conserve with vodka and Cassis or Blackcurrant Conserve with Cointreau and Cassis.
* Make half the quantity and use to sandwich a light sponge cake for a special afternoon tea.

Mandarin, Pear and Ginger Cake

A sticky, but fresh-tasting cake perfect for a hot summer's afternoon tea. Combine it with a large pitcher of iced lemonade or ginger beer for a refreshing change.

Makes 18 slices

ingredients

9 small pears, peeled and cored
Juice of ½ lemon
350 g (12 oz) plain flour
2 tsp ground cinnamon
¼ tsp ground allspice
¼ tsp freshly ground black
  pepper
1 tsp bicarbonate of soda
4 tbsp milk
100 g (3½ oz) Bonne Maman
  Mandarin Marmalade
100 g (3½ oz) black treacle
175 g (6 oz) golden syrup
175 g (6 oz) light muscovado
  sugar
175 g (6 oz) butter
5 cm (2 inch) piece of fresh
  ginger, peeled and grated
50 g (2 oz) medium oatmeal
2 large eggs

method

Preheat the oven to 170°C (fan oven 150°C), gas mark 3.

Line a 20 cm (8 inch) square by 5 cm (2 inch) deep cake tin with non-stick baking parchment. Keep the pears in a bowl of water with a squeeze of lemon juice until needed.

Put the flour and spices into a large bowl. In a cup, mix the bicarbonate of soda with the milk and set aside. Mix 2 tablespoons of the marmalade with 1 tablespoon of the black treacle, then set aside.

Place the remaining marmalade in a pan with the remaining treacle and the syrup, sugar, butter and ginger. Pour in 150 ml (¼ pint) water and heat gently until melted.

Beat the marmalade mixture into the spiced flour along with the oatmeal followed by the eggs and milk. Pour a thin layer of the cake mixture over the base of the tin and bake in the preheated oven for 10 minutes.

Drain the pears. Take the tin out of the oven and push the pears into the base. Pour the remaining cake mixture around them and return to the oven for 1 hour and 25 minutes.

Warm the reserved marmalade and treacle mixture in a small saucepan and brush over the hot cake to glaze. Serve warm or cold.

Poached Peaches with Rose Water and Raspberry

When peaches are plentiful at the end of summer, poach them in this light, fragrant syrup and watch them turn a wonderful translucent pink.

Serves 6

ingredients

300 ml (½ pint) pink zinfandel or
   rosé wine
8 tbsp Bonne Maman Raspberry
   Conserve
75 g (3 oz) golden caster sugar
2–3 drops of rose water
6 ripe peaches

to serve

Bonne Maman Galettes
Single cream

method

Put all the ingredients, except the peaches in a wide, deep pan. Heat gently until the conserve has melted, then bring to the boil. Bubble gently for 7–10 minutes until syrupy. Strain the syrup into a bowl, rinse out the pan and return the strained syrup to the clean pan.

Put the peaches in the syrup and simmer very gently for about 10 minutes, turning occasionally with a wooden spoon. Leave to cool, then remove the fruit and slip off the skins – they will come away easily.

Put the peeled peaches in a large glass serving bowl and pour over the syrup. Leave to cool, then chill for at least 1 hour.

Serve the whole fruit in individual glasses with Bonne Maman Galettes and some chilled single cream.

COOK'S TIPS

* Make the peaches up to 3–4 hours ahead and keep chilled. Any longer and the fruit begins to lose its beautiful colour.
* The peaches can be halved and stoned before poaching but look much prettier served whole. Serve the fruit with a spoon and a fork so each diner can pull the poached flesh away from the peach stone.

Peach and Almond Cupcakes

These light and fruity cupcakes are ideal to prepare as a weekend treat for a breakfast or brunch with family and friends.

Makes 12

ingredients

- 125 g (4 oz) unsalted butter, softened
- 125 g (4 oz) caster sugar
- 125 g (4 oz) self-raising flour
- 50 g (2 oz) ground almonds
- 2 large eggs
- 1 tbsp milk (optional)
- 12 tsp Bonne Maman Peach Conserve
- 50 g (2 oz) flaked almonds

method

Preheat the oven to 200°C (fan oven 180°C), gas mark 6. Line a 12-bun muffin tin with 12 muffin cases.

Put the butter, caster sugar, flour, ground almonds and eggs into a large bowl. Whisk together with an electric whisk (mixer or hand-held), or by hand, until smooth and the mixture has a dropping consistency; add the milk, if needed.

Divide the mixture between the 12 muffin cases, flattening the centre of each one. Put 1 teaspoon of peach conserve on top of each slightly indented centre, then sprinkle with some flaked almonds.

Bake in the preheated oven for 15–20 minutes. When golden brown and cooked, remove the cupcakes from the oven and cool on a wire rack. The conserve will have dropped to the centre of each cake creating a nice peachy surprise.

COOK'S TIP

* The cupcakes will keep in an airtight container for up to 3 days.

The perfect favour for a summer wedding.

Lavender Buttermilk Scones

A twist on the classic cream tea, these buttery scones have a special lavender-infused flavour and are a perfect match for any Bonne Maman® Conserve.

Makes about 12 scones

ingredients

225 g (8 oz) self-raising flour, plus extra for dusting

1 tsp baking powder

50 g (2 oz) unsalted butter, cut into small cubes, plus extra for greasing

75 g (3 oz) lavender-flavoured sugar, sifted if preferred (see Cook's Tip below)

150 ml (¼ pint) buttermilk, plus extra for brushing

Salt

Your choice of Bonne Maman Conserve, to serve

method

Preheat the oven to 220°C (fan oven 200°C), gas mark 7.

Sift the flour and baking powder into a bowl and rub in the butter until the mixture resembles breadcrumbs.

Stir in the lavender sugar (sifted if preferred) and a pinch of salt and make a well in the centre of the flour mixture. Pour in the buttermilk and mix to combine, making a soft dough.

Briefly knead the dough on a floured surface, then lightly roll out to about 2 cm (¾ inch) thick. Cut scones with a 6 cm (2½ inch) pastry cutter and place on a greased baking sheet.

Brush the top of each scone with a little extra buttermilk and bake in the preheated oven for 12–15 minutes, until lightly browned on the top. Cool on a wire rack, dust lightly with flour and serve with your favourite choice of Bonne Maman Conserve.

COOK'S TIPS

* To make lavender-flavoured sugar, push 2–3 small washed and dried sprigs of fresh lavender into a jar of caster sugar. Leave for at least 24 hours before using.

* Any flavoured sugar can be used in the scones; try cinnamon and serve the scones with Raspberry Conserve and clotted cream.

* If you cannot find buttermilk use some sour whole milk instead.

* Brushing the scones with beaten egg before baking will give them a shiny golden top.

automne
autumn

Steamed Salmon with Spiced Beetroot and Dill

You can make these parcels the day before, then chill until you're ready to cook, making it a perfect hassle-free supper for friends.

Serves 6

ingredients

350 g (12 oz) raw beetroot, trimmed but not peeled
6 tbsp olive oil
175 g (6 oz) basmati and wild rice
4 tbsp Bonne Maman Blackcurrant Conserve
Juice of 2 large lemons
3 shallots, finely chopped
6 salmon fillets, weighing about 150 g (5 oz) each, skin on
3 tbsp chopped fresh dill
Salt and freshly ground black pepper

to serve

Soured cream
Lime wedges

method

Preheat the oven to 200°C (fan oven 180°C), gas mark 6. Cut 6 large sheets of non-stick baking parchment about 30 cm (12 inches) square.

Put the beetroot on a large sheet of foil and drizzle over 1 tablespoon of the olive oil with plenty of seasoning. Scrunch the foil into a 'bag', so that the beetroot is completely sealed, and cook in the preheated oven for 1 hour or until the beetroot is very tender.

Meanwhile, cook the basmati and wild rice according to the packet instructions. Drain well and leave to cool.

Whisk together 4 tablespoons of the remaining olive oil with the conserve and lemon juice and season well.

Peel and dice the cooked beetroot and stir into the blackcurrant mixture. Fry the shallots in the remaining olive oil until soft and golden and add to the beetroot.

Season the salmon with plenty of salt and pepper. Increase the heat under the pan and add the salmon, skin side down, for 1 minute to brown, then remove from the pan and leave to cool.

Fork the beetroot mixture through the cooked rice with the dill and divide between the cut sheets of parchment. Top with the salmon and crunch the paper to form a 'bag'. Tie with fine string to seal.

Place the parcels on a baking sheet and cook in the oven for 12–15 minutes, depending on the thickness of the fillets. Serve immediately with soured cream and lime wedges.

COOK'S TIPS

* Make the parcels up to 1 day ahead. Allow 10 minutes at room temperature before cooking.
* The rice and beetroot mixture makes a delicious salad on its own and would be good served with cold poached salmon or trout and a dill-flavoured mayonnaise.

Griddled Halloumi and Tomato Salad with Pickled Cherries

Halloumi is often eaten in the summer griddled on a sizzling barbecue, but the addition of this spiced cherry sauce gives this dish a real autumnal warmth.

Serves 6

ingredients

2 tbsp olive oil, plus a little extra for brushing

1 tbsp red wine or balsamic vinegar

250 g (9 oz) rocket or soft salad leaves

1 large carrot, finely grated or shredded

A small handful of fresh thyme leaves

2 x 250 g packs halloumi cheese

3 plum tomatoes, halved

3 garlic cloves, thinly sliced

Salt and freshly ground black pepper

for the pickled cherries

400 g (14 oz) Bonne Maman Cherry Compote

½ tsp salt

2 tbsp cider vinegar

1 small garlic clove, crushed

1 large green chilli, deseeded and finely chopped

method

First make the pickled cherries: place all the ingredients in a saucepan, bring to the boil, reduce the heat and simmer gently for 10 minutes until blended and thickened. Keep warm if serving hot.

To make the dressing, whisk the olive oil, vinegar and some salt and pepper together.

In a large bowl, mix together the rocket, carrot and thyme and toss in the dressing. Set aside.

Cut each cheese into 6 slices, making 12 in total. Heat a griddle pan until hot and brush the cheese slices and halved tomatoes with a little olive oil. Sprinkle with the garlic

Place the tomato halves onto the hot griddle and cook for about 2 minutes, until singed. Turn over and cook for another 2–3 minutes.

Add the halloumi slices to the griddle pan and cook for about 2–3 minutes on each side until lightly browned. Place 2 slices of halloumi onto each serving plate. Add a tomato half, some griddled garlic and some of the rocket salad. Serve immediately with the pickled cherries.

COOK'S TIPS

* The same salad and cherries are delicious served with toasted goats' cheese or slices of buffalo mozzarella.

* Serve the pickled cherries with hot gammon or cold smoked ham.

Poussin with Peach and Herb Relish

Roasted, barbecued or pan-fried, poussin are very quick to cook and extremely moist and tender. Serve them warm with a fresh, fruity relish and a soft green salad for a memorable lunch or supper.

Serves 4

ingredients

Grated zest and juice of 1 small
   orange
4 tbsp Bonne Maman Peach
   Conserve
1 tbsp chopped mixed fresh
   parsley and mint
25 g (1 oz) butter
2 spatchcocked poussin, i.e. the
   backbone has been cut out
   and the birds flattened out
Olive oil, for brushing
2 ripe nectarines or peaches
1 tbsp white wine vinegar
3 spring onions, sliced
Salt and freshly ground black
   pepper
Green salad, to serve

method

In a small bowl, beat the orange zest, 1 tablespoon of the conserve and 1 teaspoon of the herbs with the butter. Gently ease the breast skin of the poussin away from the flesh, push in half of the butter and spread it evenly under the skin. Smooth the skin down again and brush the poussin with olive oil. Season well. Repeat with the second poussin.

Cut the nectarines or peaches into small dice and mix with the remaining conserve, vinegar, spring onions, orange juice and remaining herbs. Cover and chill until needed.

Preheat the oven to 200°C (fan oven 180°C), gas mark 6.

Heat a griddle pan or large frying pan and brown the poussin all over for 10–12 minutes. Transfer to the preheated oven and cook for a further 20 minutes. Halve the poussin down the breast bone and serve warm with the relish and a green salad.

COOK'S TIPS

* To make this dish ahead of time, prepare the relish and poussin the day before it's needed and keep chilled. Remove the poussin from the fridge about 15 minutes before cooking.
* Use the flavoured butter in the same way with chicken fillets. Roast for 30 minutes and serve as above.
* Once the poussin is cooked they are very easy to cut in half with a strong pair of scissors.

Braised Ruby Red Cabbage

Rich and comforting, this dish is perfect served simply with a baked potato or as part of a big Sunday roast dinner.

Serves 4–6

ingredients

75 g (3 oz) unsalted butter

1 kg (2¼ lb) red cabbage, finely shredded and centre core discarded

400 g (14 oz) red onions, finely sliced

2 garlic cloves, crushed

2 tsp ground ginger

1 tsp ground cinnamon

5 tbsp red wine vinegar

3 tbsp Bonne Maman Raspberry Conserve (or Jelly)

Salt and freshly ground black pepper

method

Preheat the oven to 150°C (fan oven 130°C), gas mark 2.

Melt the butter in a lidded ovenproof dish and add the cabbage, onions and garlic. Mix well and cook on the hob over a gentle heat for about 5 minutes.

Stir in the ginger and cinnamon and cook for another 3–5 minutes.

Add the red wine vinegar and the conserve, stir, and bring to the boil. Cover the casserole and transfer to the preheated oven for 3–3½ hours, stirring occasionally and adding a little hot water if necessary.

COOK'S TIPS

∗ This dish is perfect to serve with the Christmas turkey. Stir in 225 g (8 oz) cooked, peeled chestnuts for the last 30 minutes of cooking time.

∗ Braised red cabbage freezes well. Thaw overnight in the fridge and reheat on the hob, stirring, for 10–12 minutes until piping hot.

Roasted Root Vegetables with Crispy Garlic Crumbs

This is a lovely way of serving autumn root vegetables and you can use any combination. Cut the vegetables into the same-sized pieces so that they roast at the same rate.

Serves 6

ingredients

500 g (1 lb 2 oz) parsnips
500 g (1 lb 2 oz) carrots
50 ml (2 fl oz) chicken or
  vegetable stock
4 tbsp olive oil
3 tbsp Bonne Maman Apricot
  Conserve
3–4 slices garlic bread, baked
  and cooled
Juice of ½ lemon
2 tbsp chopped fresh parsley
Salt and freshly ground black
  pepper

method

Preheat the oven to 200°C (fan oven 180°C), gas mark 6.

Peel the vegetables and cut into long thin shards. Put them in a roasting tin just large enough to hold the vegetables in an even layer. Pour over the stock, cover with foil and cook in the preheated oven for 15 minutes.

Meanwhile, whisk together the olive oil and conserve with plenty of seasoning. Crumble the garlic bread into a food processor or blender and whizz into rough breadcrumbs.

Uncover the vegetables and pour off most of the stock (reserve for making gravy if serving with a roast). Stir in the conserve mixture and return to the oven for a further 20 minutes or until the vegetables are tender and golden.

Add a squeeze of lemon juice to taste, stir in the garlicky breadcrumbs and parsley and serve straight away.

COOK'S TIPS

* To make in advance, prepare the vegetables and keep covered with cold water up to 1 day ahead. Put the garlic crumbs into a bag and keep chilled. To use, drain the vegetables and cook as above.

* These roasted vegetables go perfectly with Slow Roast Belly of Pork (see page 146).

Spice it up

Make a bold style statement with this simple but effective idea for storing herbs and spices. Jars filled with the different colours and shapes of favourite flavourings such as cinnamon sticks, mace, pink peppercorns and cloves will give a unique look and ambience to a kitchen.

Simply attach Bonne Maman lids to the underside of a shelf, fill the jars and screw in place for an eye-catching and easy-to-use kitchen feature.

Duck Breasts with Mandarin Marmalade Sauce

The depth of flavour of duck meat goes perfectly with this zingy orange sauce and is perfectly balanced by some fresh green vegetables.

Serves 2

ingredients

2 duck breasts, weighing about 175–225 g (6–8 oz) each, skin on and scored

2 tbsp freshly squeezed orange or mandarin juice

3 tbsp Bonne Maman Mandarin Marmalade

1 tbsp olive oil

Salt and freshly ground pepper

method

Preheat the oven to 200°C (fan oven 180°C), gas mark 6.

Heat a heavy pan without any fat for a few minutes until very hot. Add the duck breasts, skin side down, and cook for 5–6 minutes until the skin is crisp and golden brown.

Turn the breasts over and transfer them to a roasting tin. Place in the centre of the preheated oven and cook for about 10 minutes. Remove and leave to rest on a warm dish.

While the duck is resting, place the juice and the marmalade in a pan. Heat gently until the marmalade has melted and stir in the oil. Season to taste.

Slice the duck breasts diagonally, place on warm plates and pour over the marmalade sauce.

COOK'S TIP

* Serve with herby mixed rice and some lightly cooked French beans and fresh peas.

Sausage and Garlic Bean Pot

There can be few better dishes to come home to on a chilly autumn evening than this simple, but hearty, supper.

Serves 6

ingredients

12 fat Toulouse sausages
1 tbsp olive oil
4 small red onions, finely
   chopped
300 ml (½ pint) chicken or
   vegetable stock
300 ml (½ pint) Guinness
1 x 350 g tub chilled Napoletana
   pasta sauce
2 x 410 g tins haricot beans in
   water, drained
6 tbsp Bonne Maman
   Blackcurrant Conserve
125 g (4 oz) ready-to-cook garlic
   bread slices
Chopped fresh parsley, to serve

method

Preheat the oven to 190°C (fan oven 170°C), gas mark 5. Pinch the centre of each sausage and twist the skin to form 2 smaller sausages. Cut in half to separate them. You should now have 24 small sausages.

Heat the oil in an ovenproof casserole and fry the sausages for 3–4 minutes until well browned all over. Remove with a slotted spoon and set aside.

Add the onions to the pan with no extra oil and fry for 7–10 minutes until soft and golden.

Return the sausages to the dish and stir in the stock, Guinness, pasta sauce, beans and conserve. Bring to the boil and bubble for 2 minutes, then simmer, uncovered, in the preheated oven for 40–60 minutes, or until the liquid is thickened and well reduced.

Pop the garlic bread into the oven alongside the casserole dish for the first 15 minutes of cooking time until the bread is crisp and golden. Whizz in a food processor or blender to make rough garlicky crumbs.

Serve the bean pot straight from the oven sprinkled with the garlicky crumbs and some chopped parsley.

COOK'S TIPS

* The bean pot can be made 1 day ahead but reduce the cooking time to 30 minutes only. Cover and keep chilled or freeze. When ready to use, return to room temperature and bring to the boil. Finish cooking in the oven for 15 minutes and serve with the garlicky crumbs as before.
* Make a vegetarian version of the bean pot by replacing the sausages with 700 g (1½ lb) chestnut mushrooms.
* Any coarse-textured, garlicky sausages can be used for this recipe.

Mint and Blueberry Glazed Lamb

This glaze can be used for any cut of lamb and is also good brushed onto gammon or pork joints before cooking.

Serves 6

ingredients

- 1 boned leg of lamb, weighing about 1.5 kg (3¼ lb), tied and ready to roast
- 2 tbsp olive oil
- 1 garlic clove, crushed
- 100 ml (3½ fl oz) chicken or vegetable stock

for the glaze

- 300 ml (½ pint) pomegranate juice
- 5 tbsp Bonne Maman Wild Blueberry Conserve
- 25 g (1 oz) fresh mint, roughly chopped
- 1 tbsp white wine vinegar

method

Put all the glaze ingredients into a saucepan and stir over a gentle heat until the conserve has melted. Bring to the boil and bubble for a good 5 minutes or until the liquid has reduced by about a quarter. Leave to cool completely, then strain.

Preheat the oven to 220°C (fan oven 200°C), gas mark 7.

Sit the lamb in a roasting tin just large enough to hold it comfortably. Rub all over with the olive oil and garlic. Pour the stock into the tin and put the lamb in the preheated oven to roast for about 30 minutes.

Reduce the oven temperature to 190°C (fan oven 170°C), gas mark 5 and pour over the glaze mixture. Continue to roast for a further 45 minutes, basting with the pan juices every 15 minutes.

Remove from the oven and lift onto a board for carving. Cover with foil and allow to rest for about 10–15 minutes before serving.

COOK'S TIPS

* The glaze can be made 2–3 days ahead and kept in the fridge in a jar.
* If you prefer your lamb well done, lower the oven temperature further to 170°C (fan oven 150°C), gas mark 3, cover loosely with a sheet of foil and cook for a further 1 hour.
* Stir in a little extra freshly chopped mint and you can use the glaze cold to serve as a sauce with plain grilled lamb cutlets.

Stuffed Woodland Mushrooms

Even meat-eaters will enjoy these quickly prepared and cooked mushrooms, which are delicious served with a crisp mixed salad.

Serves 4 as a starter or 2 for lunch

ingredients

1 tbsp olive oil, plus extra for greasing
4 large field mushrooms
50 g (2 oz) wholemeal breadcrumbs
2 spring onions, finely chopped
1 tbsp Bonne Maman Woodland Berries Conserve
1 tbsp chopped fresh thyme
50 g (2 oz) mature Cheddar cheese, grated
Salt and freshly ground black pepper
Mixed salad leaves, to serve

method

Preheat the oven to 200°C (fan oven 180°C), gas mark 6.

Place the mushrooms on an oiled baking sheet.

Put the wholemeal breadcrumbs, spring onions, olive oil, conserve and thyme into a bowl and thoroughly blend together. Stir in the grated cheese and add salt and pepper to taste.

Divide the stuffing between the mushrooms, pressing it down in the centres. Bake in the preheated oven for 15–20 minutes, or until the mushrooms are cooked and the stuffing has a crisp and golden top. Serve on a bed of mixed salad leaves.

COOK'S TIPS

* As an alternative, omit the Cheddar cheese and spread the mushrooms with 50 g (2 oz) soft goats' cheese. Top with the breadcrumb mixture and continue as above.
* Stir some chopped, toasted walnuts into the breadcrumbs.
* The mushrooms can be stuffed and kept chilled up to 1 day ahead of time.

Pork and Butternut Squash Casserole

A real hearty dish for an autumnal evening – or perfect for a Halloween party served in small bowls with hunks of fresh bread.

Serves 4

ingredients

2 tbsp plain flour
A large pinch of dried chilli flakes
900 g (2 lb) shoulder of pork, diced
6 tbsp vegetable oil
1 onion, chopped
1 garlic clove, sliced
2 carrots, peeled and sliced
1 butternut squash, peeled and sliced
300 ml (½ pint) chicken stock
3 tbsp Bonne Maman Peach Conserve
2–3 tbsp freshly chopped coriander
Salt and freshly ground pepper

method

Preheat the oven to 150°C (fan oven 130°C), gas mark 2.

Mix together the flour with some salt, pepper and the chilli flakes and use your fingers to rub all over the pork.

Place half the vegetable oil in a large cast-iron casserole and brown the meat in batches over a high heat. Remove the meat from the pan with a slotted spoon, add the remaining oil, then fry the onion until softened. Add the garlic and continue cooking for 1 minute.

Return the meat to the pan and add the carrots and the squash. Add the stock and bring to the boil.

Transfer to the centre of the preheated oven for 2–2½ hours or until the meat is very tender.

Remove from the oven, stir in the conserve and then adjust the seasoning. Stir in the fresh coriander and serve straight away.

COOK'S TIPS

* The casserole can be cooked up to 1 day ahead. Cool and keep chilled. When ready to use, bring the casserole to the boil on the hob and simmer very gently until piping hot.
* The casserole is delicious served on a bed of brown basmati rice.
* Mix together equal quantities of Bonne Maman Peach Conserve and mango chutney to accompany the casserole.

Storage made simple

Everyone has their favourite breakfast muesli recipe. A selection of ingredients for each person to create their own preferred assortment becomes easy once the storage potential of Bonne Maman jars is harnessed.

Use the larger compote jars to store the oats, bran and flakes. Keep mixed nuts, seeds, dried fruit and a medley of different toppings in the standard jars and allow everyone to pick and choose their own perfect recipe. Just add some fresh fruit, a spoonful of Bonne Maman compote, some milk or yogurt and voila! – a great way to start the day.

Rib-eye Steak with Mushroom and Wild Blueberry Sauce

Rich and fruity, this sauce is easy to make and perfect with pan-fried steak or game. Alternatively, make double the quantity and serve alongside a baked, smoked gammon or roast leg of lamb on another occasion.

Serves 4

ingredients

300 g (11 oz) baby button
 onions, peeled and trimmed
 but root end left intact
2 garlic cloves, sliced
300 ml (½ pint) chicken or
 vegetable stock
25 g (1 oz) butter
1–2 tbsp olive oil
150 g (5 oz) mixed exotic
 mushrooms (such as enoki,
 chestnut or shiitake), trimmed
1 tsp plain flour
5 tbsp port
2 tbsp Bonne Maman Wild
 Blueberry Conserve
Lemon juice, to taste
4 thick rib-eye steaks, weighing
 about 175–225 g (6–8 oz) each
Salt and freshly ground black
 pepper

to finish

Crispy frites
Leafy watercress salad

method

Halve any large onions, leave the rest small and put in a small saucepan with the garlic and stock. Simmer for 10 minutes, then drain, reserving the liquid.

Heat the butter with 1 tablespoon of the olive oil in a frying pan and fry the mushrooms until they are golden brown and no liquid remains; this will take a good 10 minutes. Remove from the pan with a slotted spoon and set aside.

Add the onions and garlic to the pan. Stir over the heat for 2–3 minutes until golden, then sprinkle in the flour. Cook, stirring, for 1 minute before adding the port, conserve and 100 ml (3½ fl oz) of the reserved cooking liquid. Bring to the boil and bubble for 2–3 minutes until reduced and sticky.

Return all the mushrooms to the pan, add a little lemon juice to taste with plenty of seasoning and set aside.

Brush the steaks with oil and season well. Heat a large frying pan or griddle pan over a high heat for 2 minutes, then cook the steaks for 3–4 minutes on each side for medium rare (adjust the cooking time for rare or well done). Transfer the steaks to a warm plate and leave to rest for 5 minutes while you reheat the sauce.

Pour any steak juices from the pan into the wild blueberry sauce, reheat gently for 1–2 minutes, then serve with the steaks. Accompany with crispy frites and a leafy watercress salad.

COOK'S TIPS

* The sauce can be made the day before it's needed, but bubble to reduce for 1–2 minutes only. Keep the fried mushrooms separately in the fridge. When ready to use, bring the sauce to the boil and simmer gently to reheat and reduce further. Stir in the mushrooms and lemon juice as above.
* Make sure you get a good golden colour on the mushrooms, onions and garlic for the best flavour and colour in the finished sauce.

Oven-baked Chicken with Maple Barbecue Sauce

Chicken thighs are the best part of the chicken for long, slow cooking in the oven. They are moist and full of flavour and it's virtually impossible to over cook them!

Serves 4

ingredients

2–3 tbsp oil

8 chicken thighs, skinned and boned

Salt and freshly ground black pepper

for the barbecue sauce

1 large onion, finely chopped

1 garlic clove, crushed

1 celery stick, finely chopped

½ tsp fennel seeds

½ tsp finely chopped red chilli or chilli flakes

4 tbsp Bonne Maman Blackcurrant Conserve

3 tbsp soy sauce

2 tbsp maple syrup

2 tbsp red wine vinegar

2 tbsp tomato ketchup

method

To make the sauce, heat 1 tablespoon of the oil in a medium saucepan and gently fry the onion, garlic, celery, fennel seeds and chilli in a medium saucepan until very soft and golden – this will take a good 10 minutes.

Stir in the remaining sauce ingredients and bring to the boil. Simmer very gently for 10–15 minutes, then leave to cool. Whizz the sauce in a food processor or blender until smooth, then transfer to a jar and store in the fridge until ready to use.

Preheat the oven to 170°C (fan oven 150°C), gas mark 3.

Season the chicken. Heat the remaining oil in a flameproof casserole and brown, a few pieces at a time.

Pour over the barbecue sauce and bring to the boil. Cover and cook in the preheated oven for 30 minutes. Uncover, stir, and continue to cook for a further 15–20 minutes or until tender, sticky and golden.

COOK'S TIPS

* Up to 1 day ahead of time, cook the chicken to the end of the recipe but don't uncover. Cool and keep in the fridge. To use, preheat the oven to 180°C (fan oven 160°C), gas mark 4. Bring the chicken to the boil, then reheat in the oven, uncovered, for 15–20 minutes or until piping hot and golden. Add a little extra stock if necessary.
* This sauce is so easy to make and can be kept in the fridge ready to brush over food before grilling or served cold like a ketchup with homemade burgers or sausages. It makes about 150 ml (¼ pint) but why not double the recipe and freeze some.

Roasted Potato Salad with Apricot Chilli Mayonnaise

Baby salad potatoes are delicious boiled until tender, then split and roasted until crispy and golden. Serve them hot with a sweet chilli mayonnaise. Perfect as part of a buffet meal or with any smoked meats.

Serves 4–6

ingredients

750 g (1¾ lb) baby salad
  potatoes
1 tbsp olive oil
75 g (3 oz) blanched hazelnuts,
  roughly chopped

for the mayonnaise

1 tbsp olive oil
1 onion, finely chopped
½ red chilli, deseeded and
  chopped
1 fat garlic clove, crushed
1 tsp ground coriander
175 ml (6 fl oz) white wine
2 tbsp Bonne Maman Apricot
  Conserve
300 g (11 oz) homemade or
  bought 'real' mayonnaise
125 g (4 oz) Greek yogurt
A small handful of chopped
  coriander or parsley
Salt and freshly ground black
  pepper

method

First, start the mayonnaise. Heat the olive oil in a small frying pan and fry the onion, chilli and garlic together gently for 7–10 minutes or until the onion is soft. Stir in the coriander and fry for a further minute. Add the wine and conserve, bring to the boil and then simmer for about 10 minutes. Season and leave to cool.

Preheat the oven to 200°C (fan oven 180°C), gas mark 6.

Cook the potatoes in boiling, salted water for 10–15 minutes or until very tender. Drain well and tip into a roasting tin. Split open the potatoes, drizzle over the olive oil and roast in the preheated oven for 10 minutes.

Sprinkle over the blanched hazelnuts and return to the oven for a further 10–15 minutes or until the potatoes are golden brown and very crispy and the nuts toasted.

Meanwhile, tip the cooled chilli mixture into a food processor or blender and blitz until smooth. Put the mayonnaise and yogurt together in a bowl and gradually stir in the chilli mixture, about a tablespoon at a time, until the mayonnaise is to your taste. Fold in the chopped herbs, adjust the seasoning to taste and keep chilled.

Serve the warm nutty potatoes with a generous spoonful of the chilled apricot chilli mayonnaise.

COOK'S TIPS

* The mayonnaise will keep, covered, in the fridge for up to 1 week.
* The apricot chilli mayonnaise is also good served with crispy plantain. Wash and peel 1 yellow plantain. Trim off 1 cm (½ inch) from each end, then thickly slice and fry for 2–3 minutes until crispy. Drain on kitchen paper and serve hot with the mayonnaise. Alternatively, serve the mayonnaise with thick char-grilled slices of aubergine.

Berry Crumble Cheesecake

This is one of the most rewarding puddings to make for a special occasion. Take your time in the kitchen and enjoy making this indulgent, prepare-ahead recipe.

Serves 8–10

ingredients

8 tbsp Bonne Maman Strawberry
Conserve

Finely grated zest and juice of
1 orange

150 g (5 oz) blackberries

75 g (3 oz) butter

100 g (3½ oz) golden caster
sugar

40 g (1½ oz) plain flour

25 g (1 oz) crunchy baked
granola-style cereal

2 x 90 g packets Bonne Maman
Galettes, finely crushed

150 g (5 oz) mild creamy goats'
cheese

450 g (1 lb) full-fat soft cheese

4 large eggs

75 ml (3 fl oz) soured cream
(about 5 tablespoons)

Icing sugar, to dust

method

Preheat the oven to 180°C (fan oven 160°C), gas mark 4. Line the base and sides of a deep, 20 cm (8 inch), loose-based, springform cake tin with greaseproof paper.

Put the conserve in a small saucepan with 50 ml (2 fl oz) of the orange juice and stir over a low heat. Bring to the boil and bubble gently for 5 minutes until reduced by about half. Add in the blackberries and leave to cool.

Rub 25 g (1 oz) of the butter and 25 g (1 oz) of the caster sugar into the flour. Stir in the granola cereal and spread out on a foil-lined baking sheet. Bake in the preheated oven for 10–12 minutes until golden brown. Leave to cool, then break into rough crumbs with a fork.

Reduce the oven temperature to 170°C (fan oven 150°C), gas mark 3.

Melt the remaining butter in a small saucepan and stir in the crushed biscuits. Press the crumbs over the base of the lined tin and set aside.

Beat together the cheeses, eggs, orange zest and remaining sugar with the soured cream until smooth. Spoon onto the biscuit base and bake for 1¼ hours in the oven.

Open the oven door and pull the cheesecake out a little. Drizzle the blackberries and their liquid randomly over the surface and return to the oven for a further 1–1¼ hours until the cheesecake feels just firm when touched in the centre.

Sprinkle over the crumble mixture, leave to cool and dust with icing sugar before serving.

COOK'S TIPS

* The cheesecake can be made ahead and kept in the fridge for up to 3 days without the crumble topping. It also freezes well.
* Mixing goats' cheese with the soft cheese gives a slight acidity to the filling, which offsets the richness. However, it can be omitted – just use 600 g (1 lb 6 oz) full-fat soft cheese.

Almond Crêpes with Plums in Thyme and Blackcurrant Syrup

These crêpes make a perfect light dessert to end any special meal and the rich and sticky syrup gives it a real fruity kick.

Serves 4

for the plums in syrup

6 tbsp Bonne Maman
  Blackcurrant Conserve
Juice of 1 orange
2 tbsp light soft brown sugar
1 tbsp fresh thyme leaves, tied
  in muslin
150 ml (¼ pint) red wine
250 g (9 oz) small plums, halved
  and stoned

for the crêpes

50 g (2 oz) butter, melted, plus
  extra for cooking
100 g (3½ oz) plain flour
1 large egg and 1 egg yolk
300 ml (½ pint) milk
1 tbsp caster sugar
150 g (5 oz) toasted flaked
  almonds

for the filling

1 x 200 ml tub mascarpone
  cheese
1 x 150 ml carton double cream
1 tsp orange zest
Icing sugar, to dust

method

Simmer all the plum ingredients together for 10–12 minutes or until the plums are just tender.

To make the crêpes, whisk together the melted butter, flour, egg and egg yolk, milk and sugar with 50 ml (2 fl oz) cold water. Heat an 18–20 cm (7–8 inch) crêpe pan and brush lightly with melted butter.

Sprinkle 1 tablespoon flaked almonds into the crêpe pan then pour in 50–75 ml (2–3 fl oz) of the mixed batter. Tilt the pan so that the batter runs all over the surface.

Cook for 1 minute until the underside is golden, flip over and cook for a further 1 minute. Tip the crêpe onto a plate. Continue until you have used all the batter.

Stir together the filling ingredients, spread over the pancakes and roll up. Dust with icing sugar and serve with the warm plums in syrup.

COOK'S TIPS

∗ Make the crêpes the day before and store in an airtight container. Wrap in foil and warm in a low oven for 10 minutes before using.

∗ The crêpes are also delicious served with blackberries. Omit the plums, use the same quantity of blackberries and simmer for 5 minutes only.

∗ Add a good pinch of ground nutmeg to the crêpe batter for a hint of fragrant spice.

*Enjoy peaceful painting using Bonne Maman.®
jars for storing brushes and pencils.*

Strawberry and Wild Strawberry Vodka Granita

A refreshing pudding to serve after a spicy main course. Vary the alcohol depending on what you have to hand – orange-based liqueurs and Crème de Cassis work well too.

Serves 4

ingredients

1 x 370 g jar Bonne Maman
  Strawberry and Wild
  Strawberry Conserve
2 tbsp lemon juice
2 tbsp orange juice
4 tbsp vodka
Bonne Maman Galettes, to serve

method

Put the conserve, lemon juice and orange juice and 300 ml (½ pint) water in a small saucepan. Heat gently, stirring, until the conserve has melted. Leave to cool, then stir in the vodka.

Pour the mixture into a shallow freezer-proof container and put in the freezer for 1 hour. Ice crystals will have started to form around the edge of the container, so take a fork and stir them into the middle.

Return the container to the freezer for a further hour and stir in the ice crystals again. Repeat until all the liquid has frozen and the container is full of fluffy ice.

Serve in tall glasses or champagne flutes with Bonne Maman Galettes or any fine sweet biscuit.

COOK'S TIPS

* The granita can be made up to 3 hours ahead of time and eaten straight from the freezer. If frozen for any longer, remove from the freezer and allow 10–15 minutes in the fridge to soften before serving.
* Any conserve can be used to make a fruit granita in this way. However, some, such as raspberry, should be sieved before freezing to remove the fruit seeds.
* For a special occasion, omit the vodka and water and use 300 ml (½ pint) Champagne or a sparkling wine, such as Prosecco.

Apricot and Almond Mille-Feuilles

This quick but glamorous dessert will make a delicious finale to any autumnal meal and is definitely one to impress.

Serves 6

ingredients

600 g (1 lb 6 oz) chilled puff
  pastry
Flour, for dusting
A pinch of caster sugar
1 x 150 ml carton double cream,
  lightly whipped
1 x 150 ml carton crème fraîche
25 g (1 oz) toasted flaked
  almonds
2 heaped tbsp Bonne Maman
  Apricot Conserve
Icing sugar, to dust

method

Preheat the oven to 200°C (fan oven 180°C), gas mark 6.

Roll out the pastry on a lightly floured surface into a 15 x 60 cm (6 x 24 inch) rectangle, trim the edges and chill for 15 minutes.

Cut the rectangle into 3 smaller rectangles and place on baking sheets lined with non-stick baking parchment.

Prick with a fork and lightly sprinkle with the caster sugar.

Bake in the preheated oven for 12 minutes until golden. Cool on a wire rack.

Gently combine the whipped cream, crème fraîche, toasted almonds and the conserve in a large bowl.

Spread half the cream mixture onto one of the pastry rectangles, top with a second pastry rectangle and spread with the remaining cream. Cover with the last layer of pastry and dust with icing sugar to serve.

COOK'S TIPS

* The pastry can be baked up to 2 days ahead and kept, interleaved with greaseproof paper, in an airtight container.
* Assemble the mille-feuilles no more than 1 hour before serving or the pastry will begin to soften.

Raspberry Frangipane Tarts

The classic bakewell tart flavour in an individual serving – a stylish and satisfying ending to any meal or dinner party.

Serves 4

ingredients

175 g (6 oz) plain flour, plus
   extra for dusting
75 g (3 oz) butter
25 g (1 oz) caster sugar
1 egg yolk
1 tbsp almond extract

for the filling

175 g (6 oz) Bonne Maman
   Raspberry Conserve
2 large free-range eggs
150 g (5 oz) mascarpone
   cheese
75 g (3 oz) caster sugar
50 g (2 oz) ground almonds
25 g (1 oz) flaked almonds

to finish

1 tbsp icing sugar, to dust
1 x 200 ml tub crème fraîche

method

Preheat the oven to 200°C (fan oven 180°C), gas mark 6.

To make the pastry, put the flour, butter, caster sugar and egg yolk into a food processor or blender and pulse until it reaches the consistency of breadcrumbs.

Place 3 tablespoons water in a cup and stir in the almond extract. With the motor running, add enough water, a little at a time, until the mixture just begins to form a dough. Roll out the dough on a lightly floured surface and line 4 x 12 cm (5 inch) ceramic flan dishes. Prick the pastry all over with a fork and refrigerate until needed.

Bake the pastry cases blind (see page 41) in the preheated oven for about 12–15 minutes, until cooked and golden brown.

To assemble the tarts, spread the conserve over the base of the pastry cases. Separate the eggs and mix together the egg yolks, mascarpone, sugar and ground almonds. Whisk the whites in a clean, dry bowl to stiff peaks and fold into the mascarpone mixture. Pour this over the raspberry bases and top with the flaked almonds.

Reduce the oven temperature to 180°C (fan oven 160°C), gas mark 4 and bake the tarts for about 15–25 minutes.

The tarts are cooked when the tops have risen a little and the mixture is set and golden. Lightly dust with icing sugar and serve warm with a dollop of crème fraîche.

COOK'S TIP

* The tarts can be made up to 1 day ahead and kept in an airtight container. Warm in a low oven for 10 minutes before serving.

Chocolate and Vanilla Panna Cotta with Cherry Chocolate Sauce

Panna Cotta, 'cooked cream', is an Italian classic that is simple to make at home. This vanilla and chocolate combination is perfect to serve with a warm black cherry sauce.

Serves 6

ingredients

4 sheets of leaf gelatine
1 x 600 ml carton double cream
200 ml (7 fl oz) whole milk
175 g (6 oz) golden caster sugar
75 g (3 oz) good-quality plain
  chocolate, finely chopped
1 vanilla pod
8 tbsp Bonne Maman Black
  Cherry Conserve
4 tbsp dark red fruit juice, such
  as red grape or pomegranate

method

Soak the gelatine sheets in a small bowl of cold water for 5 minutes.

Mix together the cream, milk and sugar in a medium saucepan and heat gently until the sugar dissolves.

Lift the gelatine from the water, squeeze out any excess liquid and put into the pan with the cream mixture. Heat very gently for 1–2 minutes until the gelatine has dissolved.

Put 50 g (2 oz) of the chopped chocolate into a heatproof jug and pour over half of the warm cream. Stir gently to melt the chocolate.

Split the vanilla pod lengthways and scrape the seeds into the remaining cream in the saucepan.

Rinse 6 x 150 ml (¼ pint) glasses with cold water and do not dry. Divide the chocolate mixture between each glass. Sit the glasses on a tray with some coins or a piece of scrunched up foil under one side to slant the mixture as it sets. Chill for 1 hour. Keep the vanilla custard over a pan of warm water to prevent it from setting.

When the chocolate mixture has set return the glasses to upright and slowly pour on the vanilla custard. Return to the fridge for 1 hour to set.

Warm the cherry conserve with the fruit juice in a small saucepan. Bring to the boil and simmer for 2–3 minutes. Remove from the heat and stir in the remaining chocolate. Stir until the chocolate has completely melted. Leave to cool.

Serve the panna cotta chilled with some of the cherry chocolate sauce spooned on top.

COOK'S TIPS

* The panna cotta and the sauce can be made up to 3 days ahead of time. Keep, covered, in the fridge.
* The black cherry and chocolate sauce can also be served warm. Hand round a bowl of the sauce to spoon on top.
* Don't throw away the vanilla pod once the seeds have been removed. Use it to make some vanilla sugar (see pages 48–49 and 94).

Apricot and Honey Parfait

Apricot and honey are a perfect combination of flavours in this creamy ice cream. It's fast to make and very refreshing to eat.

Serves 6–8

ingredients

A little vegetable oil, for greasing
10 ratafia or amaretti biscuits
1 x 300 ml carton double cream
1 x 600 g jar Bonne Maman
   Apricot Compote
2 tbsp Kirsch or vodka
2 tbsp clear honey

method

Lightly oil a 900 g (2 lb) loaf tin and line with non-stick baking parchment. Put the biscuits in a polythene bag and crumble into large, rough pieces with the end of a rolling pin.

Whip the cream until it just begins to hold its shape – the whisk should leave a trail on the cream when lifted.

Weigh out 300 g (11 oz) of the compote and stir in the Kirsch or vodka and half the honey. Fold the compote and crumbled biscuits into the whipped cream and spoon into the lined tin. Freeze for 3–4 hours until firm.

Stir the remaining honey and compote together and set aside.

Turn out the parfait and cut into thick slices. Serve straight away with a spoonful of honeyed compote.

COOK'S TIP

∗ The parfait should be made and eaten on the same day. To make serving very simple, slice the frozen parfait into portions and lay flat on a baking sheet lined with foil or baking parchment. Return to the freezer for about 30 minutes until firm again. Cover lightly until needed.

Rhubarb and Aubergine Chutney

If you have never made homemade chutney, this recipe will prove just how simple it is. Make a large batch now and it will be matured and ready to enjoy over the next few months. Try to save some to serve with any Christmas leftovers of turkey, ham or cheeses.

Makes about 4 x 370 g jars

ingredients

900 ml (1½ pints) distilled malt vinegar

600 g (1 lb 6 oz) light soft brown sugar

700 g (1½ lb) cooking apples, peeled and roughly chopped

225 g (8 oz) dessert apples, peeled and roughly chopped

225 g (8 oz) aubergine, roughly chopped

450 g (1 lb) onions, roughly chopped

225 g (8 oz) sultanas

25 g (1 oz) English mustard powder

25 g (1 oz) fresh ginger, peeled and finely sliced

2 tsp mustard seeds

2 tsp mild garam masala

1 tsp chilli flakes (optional)

25 g (1 oz) salt

225 g (8 oz) Bonne Maman Rhubarb Compote

75 g (3 oz) walnut pieces

method

Put the vinegar and sugar into a large, non-corrosive saucepan or preserving pan and bring to the boil.

Add all the other ingredients, except the walnuts. Bring the mixture to the boil again and bubble gently, stirring regularly, until it is well reduced. This should take about 45–60 minutes but remember that the chutney will thicken up further on cooling.

Meanwhile, sterilise 4 or 5 Bonne Maman jars. Wash them in hot soapy water, rinse well and put them into a warm oven to dry. Leave the jars until you are ready to use them. Alternatively, use jars hot from the dishwasher.

Stir the walnuts into the hot chutney and spoon it into the prepared jars. Stretch a piece of cling film over the top of the jar and secure with the lid.

Store in a cool, dry place for about 4 weeks before using. Once opened, store in the fridge. Unopened chutney will keep for up to 6 months.

COOK'S TIPS

∗ The chutney needs to be stored before using. This gives the chutney ingredients time to mellow and mature. Make sure you store the jars in a cool, dry and dark place.

∗ Chutney makes a wonderful homemade gift to give to friends (see page 136). The recipe is easily doubled up, just make sure you use or hire a large, wide preserving pan as the mixture needs space to bubble gently to evaporate the liquid.

∗ If you need to make the chutney in batches, everything except the sugar and vinegar can be chopped and mixed together ready to cook.

Preserving your harvest

Autumn is the time of year to gather some home-grown produce with some exotic spices and prepare some delicious relishes for the Christmas table, or simply to enjoy over the winter months. From spiced chutneys (like the Rhubarb and Aubergine Chutney on page 135) to fiery pickles or tangy 'citrons confits' – they all look so much more stylish in the larder when packed into a selection of Bonne Maman jars.

Not only is it satisfying to fill the store cupboard but they make perfect presents as well.

Raspberry Scrunch Pie

This recipe title sums up the shape of this easy fruit pudding. It needs no special tins or dishes and no pastry skills!

Serves 6

ingredients

400 g (14 oz) ripe plums, peaches or nectarines

4 tbsp Bonne Maman Raspberry Conserve

Juice of 1 small orange

1 x 250 g pack chilled puff pastry

Flour, for dusting

150 g (5 oz) Madeira cake, thinly sliced

50 g (2 oz) white marzipan, coarsely grated

1 small egg, beaten

2 tbsp golden caster sugar

Vanilla custard, ice cream or single cream, to finish

method

Preheat the oven to 190°C (fan oven 170°C), gas mark 5.

Halve and stone the fruit. Cut into thick slices and put into a bowl. Stir in the conserve and orange juice.

Roll the pastry out thinly on a lightly floured surface to a rough circle about 25 cm (10 inches) round. Lift onto a baking sheet (it will hang over the edge but don't worry).

Lay the cake slices in an overlapping circle, roughly 18 cm (7 inches) in diameter in the centre of the pastry. Sprinkle with the marzipan and pile the fruit mixture on top.

Now, bring the edges of the puff pastry up and over the fruit, folding and pinching it as you go. The pastry won't cover all the fruit but should form a wide, roughly pleated edge.

Brush the pastry with beaten egg and sprinkle generously with the sugar.

Bake the pie in the preheated oven for 40–45 minutes or until puffed and deep golden brown. Allow to cool for 10 minutes before serving as the fruit juices become very hot.

Finish with a good ready-made hot or chilled vanilla custard, ice cream or chilled single cream.

COOK'S TIPS

* Prepare the pie to the point that it is ready to go in the oven, up to 1 day ahead. Keep loosely covered in the fridge.
* The Madeira cake soaks up the juices from the cooking fruit. Any favourite sponge can be used: try lemon drizzle cake.
* Any firm fruit and conserve can be used in this way – try sliced apple with peach conserve or pear with apricot conserve.

Apple and Caramel Crumble

This mouth-watering crumble, with its irresistible combination of flavours, will impress anyone allowed a spoonful. Enjoy preparing it for your family and friends.

Serves 6

ingredients

1 kg (2¼ lb) Golden Delicious
   apples
Juice of 1 large lemon
75 g (3 oz) toasted chopped
   pecan nuts
4 heaped tbsp Bonne Maman
   Confiture de Caramel
Vanilla ice cream or custard, to
   finish

for the topping

100 g (3½ oz) polenta
100 g (3½ oz) plain flour
75 g (3 oz) golden caster sugar
A pinch of salt
75 g (3 oz) butter, diced

method

Preheat the oven to 180 °C (fan oven 160°C), gas mark 4.

Peel and slice the apples and place them in an ovenproof dish. Gently toss in the lemon juice so that the apples are completely coated.

Sprinkle the pecan nuts over the apples, then spoon over the Confiture de Caramel, trying to cover all the fruit and nuts.

To make the topping, combine the polenta, flour, sugar and salt in a bowl. Rub in the butter until the mixture resembles breadcrumbs.

Spread over the apples and press down lightly. Bake in the preheated oven for about 35–40 minutes, then serve.

Serve the crumble hot from the oven with vanilla ice cream to melt on top. Alternatively, serve the crumble cold with warm vanilla custard.

hiver winter

Spiced Smoked Trout Kedgeree

Ease into Sunday with this simple kedgeree. It's ideal for brunch or for a quick supper that can be on the table in less than 30 minutes.

Serves 4

ingredients

125 g (4 oz) basmati rice
½ tsp ground turmeric
1 cardamom pod, split
7 tbsp Bonne Maman Apricot
  Compote
2 tbsp good-quality mango
  chutney
25 g (1 oz) butter
1 large Spanish onion, finely
  chopped
A large pinch of garam masala
Grated zest and juice of 1 large
  lemon
A small bunch of fresh coriander
  or parsley, roughly chopped
125 g (4 oz) hot smoked trout
  fillets, flaked
Salt and freshly ground black
  pepper

to finish

4 soft poached eggs
Soured cream, topped with
  chopped herbs
Lime or lemon wedges

method

Cook the basmati rice with the turmeric and cardamom in boiling, salted water for about 7–10 minutes until just tender. Drain well, return to the pan and keep covered.

Stir 3 tablespoons of the compote into the mango chutney in a small bowl and set aside.

Melt the butter in a large frying pan and cook the onion for about 7 minutes, stirring, until softened. Stir in the garam masala and the remaining compote and keep stirring over the heat for a further 5–7 minutes or until the onions are golden brown and the compote is reduced to a sticky coating.

Add the cooked rice, lemon zest and herbs to the onions and stir over a medium heat until warmed through. Gently stir in the trout, add lemon juice to taste and cover with a lid or foil to keep warm.

Top the kedgeree with a small, soft poached egg (if using) and season to taste. Have small bowls of the apricot and mango chutney, soured cream topped with some chopped herbs and lime or lemon wedges ready to hand round separately with the kedgeree.

COOK'S TIP

✳ For a Spanish twist, replace the trout and garam masala with crispy, fried chunks of chorizo sausage.

Griddled Lamb with Mediterranean Stew

This dish has a wonderful, rich mixture of flavours – and much of the preparation can be done in advance. Bring the casserole to the table and serve quite simply with chunks of warm ciabatta bread to soak up the juices and a salad of soft green leaves.

Serves 6

ingredients

3 tbsp olive oil

2 large red onions, chopped

3 garlic cloves, crushed

1 red chilli, split and deseeded

3 tsp smoked ground paprika

1 small aubergine, chopped

1 red pepper, deseeded and chopped

1 small butternut squash, chopped

300 ml (½ pint) passata

1 x 400 g tin tomatoes

300 ml (½ pint) red wine

300 ml (½ pint) chicken or vegetable stock

3 tbsp Bonne Maman Wild Blueberry Conserve

12 small lamb cutlets, about 75 g (3 oz) each

About 12 pitted black olives

Salt and freshly ground black pepper

method

Preheat the oven to 170°C (fan oven 150°C), gas mark 3.

Heat 2 tablespoons of the oil in a large casserole and add the onions and garlic. Fry over a medium heat for 7–10 minutes until the onions are soft. Stir in the chilli and 2 teaspoons of the paprika and continue to fry, stirring, for a further 1–2 minutes.

Add the aubergine, pepper and squash and stir-fry for 2–3 minutes until beginning to colour, then stir in the passata, tomatoes, red wine, stock and conserve. Bring to the boil, cover and place in the preheated oven to cook for about 1–1½ hours or until all the vegetables are tender.

Rub the lamb cutlets with the remaining paprika and brush with the leftover oil. Season lightly. Heat a griddle pan or frying pan until smoky hot and quickly brown the cutlets on all sides.

Remove the stew from the oven and uncover. Stir in the olives, then taste and adjust the seasoning, if necessary. Tuck the lamb into the vegetables and return the casserole to the oven, uncovered, for a final 10 minutes.

COOK'S TIPS

* Make the vegetable stew up to 2 days ahead and keep in the fridge. When ready to use, bring to the boil, then simmer for 10–12 minutes until piping hot and continue as above.
* The stew makes a wonderful vegetarian supper served on its own or with a bowl of steamed couscous.

Slow Roast Belly of Pork

A no-hassle roast that guarantees mouth-wateringly tender meat every time. Perfect for a winter Sunday lunch.

Serves 6–8

ingredients

1.6 kg (3½ lb) piece of belly of
  pork
500 ml (17 fl oz) medium dry
  cider
600 ml (1 pint) chicken or
  vegetable stock
2 sprigs of fresh rosemary
2 fat garlic cloves
1 tbsp olive oil
4 tsp sea salt
1 tsp dried fennel seeds
6 tbsp Bonne Maman Bitter
  Orange Marmalade
2 tsp plain flour
1 tsp butter
Salt and freshly ground black
  pepper

method

Preheat the oven to 170°C (fan oven 150°C), gas mark 3.

Put the belly of pork in a large roasting tin and add the cider, stock and rosemary. Bring to the boil on the hob, then cover tightly with foil and poach in the preheated oven for 3 hours. Leave to cool.

Meanwhile, in a pestle and mortar or a strong bowl with the end of a rolling pin, pound the garlic, olive oil, 2 teaspoons of the salt and the fennel seeds to a rough paste. Add 2 tablespoons of the marmalade and pound for a further few seconds.

Raise the oven temperature to 220°C (fan oven 200°C), gas mark 7.

Drain the pork, reserving the cooking liquid. With a sharp knife, cut away the rind from the pork fat and set it aside on a large piece of foil. Score the fat with a sharp knife.

Rinse out the roasting tin, return the meat to the tin and spread the fat with the marmalade mixture. Rub the pork rind with the remaining salt.

Put the pork in the oven, with the pork rind on a shelf above, and roast for 10 minutes. Reduce the temperature to 200°C (fan oven 180°C), gas mark 6, and continue to roast for a further 20–25 minutes until the pork is golden brown and the crackling crisp.

Meanwhile, put the poaching liquid in a large saucepan with the remaining marmalade and bring to the boil. Bubble for a good 10–15 minutes until reduced by about two-thirds.

Mash the flour into the butter and whisk into the liquid. Return to the boil, whisking all the time, and cook until lightly thickened. Adjust the seasoning to taste. Serve the pork carved into thick slices with shards of crispy crackling and the gravy.

COOK'S TIPS

* To prepare ahead of time, poach the pork for 3 hours the day before it is needed. Drain, remove the rind and make the gravy. Keep everything covered in the fridge. When ready to use, allow the pork and rind 15 minutes at room temperature before roasting. Bring the gravy to the boil and simmer for 10 minutes until piping hot.
* The pork is perfect served with Roasted Root Vegetables with Crispy Garlic Crumbs (see page 105).

Beef Steeped in Stout

Plan ahead and stock the freezer with some comforting stews so you need only thaw them and pop them in the oven when needed.

Serves 4–6

ingredients

1 kg (2¼ lb) braising steak

4 tbsp vegetable oil

450 g (1 lb) small Chanteney carrots, trimmed

2 large onions, roughly chopped

1 tbsp plain flour

1 x 330 ml bottle stout

750 ml (1¼ pints) stock (any kind)

4 tbsp Bonne Maman Blackcurrant Conserve

Salt and freshly ground black pepper

for the dumplings

1 small onion, finely chopped

A knob of butter

A small handful of fresh chives, chopped

75 g (3 oz) fresh white breadcrumbs

1 egg

2 tsp Dijon mustard

method

First make a start on the dumplings. Fry the onion in the butter and mix with all the remaining ingredients. Cover and chill for at least 1 hour to firm up.

Preheat the oven to 170°C (fan oven 150°C), gas mark 3.

Cut the steak into large bite-sized pieces. Heat 2 tablespoons of the oil in a large casserole, then fry the meat a few pieces at a time until they are a deep golden brown. Remove with a slotted spoon and set aside.

Add the remaining oil to the pan and brown the carrots and onions for 3–4 minutes until they are just beginning to colour. Stir in the flour, scraping up any crusty bits from the base of the pan.

Pour in the stout along with the stock and conserve. Return all the meat with any juices. Bring to the boil, cover tightly with a lid and simmer in the preheated oven for 2–2¼ hours or until meltingly tender.

Meanwhile, with damp hands, shape the chilled dumpling mixture into 12 small balls and return to the fridge. About 30 minutes before the end of cooking time, uncover the beef and taste the juices for seasoning. Drop the dumplings on top and return the casserole to the oven, uncovered, to continue cooking for the remaining cooking time.

COOK'S TIPS

* To make in advance, up to 2 days ahead of time, cook the beef as above but for 1½ hours only. Cool and keep in the fridge or freeze. Make the dumpling mixture and keep, covered, in the fridge. When ready to use, thaw the beef if necessary and bring to the boil on the hob, cover and place in the oven for 1 hour. Make and add the dumplings as above.
* The dumplings are optional but they are much lighter than traditional suet dumplings so don't make the dish stodgy.
* Alternatively, spread 6 thick slices of baguette with mustard and crushed garlic and pop them on top of the beef for the last 30 minutes.

Bonne Maman® mini pots are just the right size to make a novel advent calendar.

Pheasant, Bacon and Berry Casserole

The wonderful rich flavours of this dish develop even more if it's made the day before. Perfect with a big spoonful of creamy mash to soak up all the juices.

Serves 4

ingredients

15 g (½ oz) dried mushrooms
25 g (1 oz) butter
2 oven-ready pheasants, jointed
4 juniper berries, crushed
2 onions, finely chopped
125 g (4 oz) smoked streaky
   bacon lardons
1 tbsp plain flour
300 ml (½ pint) red wine
300 ml (½ pint) stock (any kind)
150 g (5 oz) button mushrooms
2 tbsp Bonne Maman Woodland
   Berries Conserve

method

Preheat the oven to 180°C (fan oven 160°C), gas mark 4.

Soak the dried mushrooms in 300 ml (½ pint) warm water for 20 minutes. Drain, reserving the liquid, and finely chop.

In a large casserole, melt the butter and brown the pheasant pieces well on all sides. Remove with a slotted spoon and set aside.

Add the juniper berries to the pan with the onions and bacon and fry gently for 10 minutes until golden.

Stir in the soaked mushrooms and flour, followed by the wine and stock. Bring to the boil, return all the pheasant pieces, cover and cook in the preheated oven for 25 minutes.

Uncover the casserole, stir in the button mushrooms, cover again and return to the oven for a further 20–25 minutes until very tender.

Using a slotted spoon, transfer the contents of the casserole to a warm platter leaving the cooking juices behind. Cover and keep warm.

Bring the cooking juices to the boil and stir in the conserve. Add a little of the mushroom soaking liquid if needed. Bubble for 1–2 minutes, then spoon over the pheasant and serve.

COOK'S TIPS

* To make this casserole ahead, cook the pheasant up to the end of the recipe the day before. Cool, cover and keep chilled. To use, return the casserole to the boil, cover and simmer very gently on the hob for 10–15 minutes or until piping hot.
* When pheasant is out of season use small guinea fowl.

Fruity Chestnut and Rice Stuffing

This stuffing is ideal for the turkey or goose at Christmas or for slipping under the skin of chicken or pheasant breasts before roasting.

Makes enough to stuff a 5.5 kg (12 lb) turkey

ingredients

- 50 g (2 oz) smoked bacon lardons
- 2 red onions, finely chopped
- 1 tbsp Bonne Maman Wild Blueberry Conserve
- 2 tbsp port, Marsala or sherry
- Coarsely grated zest of 1 small orange
- 25 g (1 oz) brown rice, cooked and drained
- 125 g (4 oz) cooked, peeled chestnuts, roughly chopped
- 2 tbsp chopped fresh parsley
- 1 tsp chopped fresh thyme
- 125 g (4 oz) coarse pork sausagemeat

method

Dry-fry the bacon lardons in a frying pan until crisp and golden. Remove with a slotted spoon and set aside.

Stir the onion into the bacon fat and cook gently, stirring, for 7–10 minutes, until golden and soft. Stir in the conserve and port, Marsala or sherry and stir over the heat until blended together. Leave to cool.

Mix all the remaining ingredients into the cold onion mixture and set aside until required.

COOK'S TIPS

* The stuffing can be made up to 2 days ahead and kept, covered, in the fridge. The stuffing will freeze if you use pork sausagemeat that has not been previously frozen. To use, thaw overnight in the fridge. Make sure you allow enough time for the stuffing to thaw before using.
* Most supermarkets now sell chopped lardons of bacon. If you cannot find them, buy 50 g (2 oz) smoked streaky bacon and cut into small strips.
* Omit the chestnuts and use chopped toasted walnuts.

Cherry and Mulled Wine Sauce

This sauce gains its intense flavour from the spices steeped in the wine overnight. It works very well with roast turkey as a change from the traditional cranberry, with cooked ham, roast pork and duck – or even as an accompaniment for venison sausages.

Makes about 150 ml (¼ pint)

ingredients

150 ml (¼ pint) red wine
Pared zest and juice of
   2 tangerines or mandarin
   oranges
2.5 cm (1 inch) piece of fresh
   ginger, peeled and sliced
1 star anise
6 generous tbsp Bonne Maman
   Black Cherry Conserve
2 tsp arrowroot

method

Put the wine, pared zest, ginger and star anise in a saucepan and bring to the boil. Cover and set aside overnight to infuse.

Strain the liquid and return to the saucepan with the cherry conserve. Warm over a gentle heat, stirring, until the conserve has melted.

Mix the tangerine or mandarin juice with the arrowroot in a cup, then stir into the pan. Bring slowly to the boil, then simmer gently for 2–3 minutes until the sauce is lightly thickened. Serve hot or cold.

COOK'S TIP

∗ The sauce can be made up to 3 days ahead and kept chilled or frozen. To use, thaw and serve at room temperature or reheat gently to serve warm.

Black Bean Chilli Pot

Make a large batch of this rich vegetable chilli and freeze ready for cold nights ahead. It's sure to become a firm family favourite.

Serves 4

ingredients

150 g (5 oz) dried black beans,
   soaked overnight in cold water
2 tbsp oil
1 large red onion, finely diced
125 g (4 oz) each of carrots and
   celery, finely chopped
1 tsp chopped red chilli
1 tsp ground turmeric
1 tsp cumin seeds
4 tbsp Bonne Maman Apricot
   Conserve
1 x 400 g tin chopped tomatoes
   with garlic
2 tbsp tomato purée
450 ml (¾ pint) stock (any kind)
1 square of plain chocolate
Salt and freshly ground black
   pepper

to finish

Grilled flatbreads
Soured cream
Chopped fresh coriander
Avocado wedges

method

Drain the beans, put them in a saucepan and cover with cold water. Bring to the boil and bubble for 10 minutes. Drain, cover with fresh water, return to the boil and simmer for 20–30 minutes until just tender. Drain.

Heat the oil in a medium saucepan and fry all the vegetables with the chilli until golden and beginning to soften. Stir in the turmeric and cumin and cook over the heat for 1 minute before adding the conserve, tomatoes, purée and stock.

Stir in the black beans, bring to the boil, cover and simmer very gently for 30–45 minutes, stirring occasionally, or until all the vegetables are tender and the liquid reduced and rich.

Mix in the square of chocolate until it is completely melted and adjust the seasoning to taste.

Finish the chilli with grilled flatbreads (see below) and bowls of soured cream, chopped coriander and avocado wedges.

COOK'S TIPS

* Cook the chilli up to 3 days ahead. Keep chilled or freeze. To use, bring to the boil, then simmer for 10–12 minutes until piping hot.
* Chocolate is a regular addition to spicy food in South America, just 1 square gives this pot a rich, smooth creaminess.
* To grill flatbreads (tortillas or wraps), cut them into thick fingers. Brush with garlic oil and toast under the grill on both sides until golden and crispy. Sprinkle with sea salt before serving.

Strawberry and Passion Fruit Brulées

The combination of strawberry and passion fruit is simply sensational and offers a delightful contrast of flavours with the rich custard.

Serves 6

ingredients

Strained juice of 2 passion fruit
6 tbsp Bonne Maman Strawberry
  Conserve
4 large egg yolks
1 tbsp golden caster sugar
Grated zest of ½ orange
½ tsp finely grated fresh ginger
1 x 600 ml carton double cream
Vegetable oil, for greasing
8 tbsp granulated sugar

method

Preheat the oven to 170°C (fan oven 150°C), gas mark 3.

Mix together the passion fruit juice and the conserve and divide between 6 x 7.5 cm (3 inch) round, 5 cm (2 inch) deep ramekin dishes or any other heatproof and freezer-proof dishes. Put the ramekins in the freezer for 1 hour or until the strawberry mixture has frozen.

With a wooden spoon, beat together the egg yolks, caster sugar, orange zest and ginger until well combined.

Put the cream in a saucepan and slowly bring to just below boiling. Immediately pour the hot cream onto the egg yolk mixture, stirring all the time with a wooden spoon. Leave to cool, then strain into a jug.

Sit the ramekins in a roasting tin. Pour the cooled custard onto the frozen sauce, then pour boiling water to come halfway up the sides of the dishes.

Cook in the preheated oven for about 25 minutes or until a skin has formed on top of the custard but it is still wobbly in the middle. Chill the ramekins overnight in the fridge.

For the brulée topping, put a sheet of oiled foil on a baking sheet. Put the granulated sugar in a small saucepan and place over a gentle heat until the sugar begins to melt and turn golden brown.

Immediately pour the caramel onto the foil and leave until cold and set. Break into a food processor or blender and whizz to form a fine powder. Tip into a clean, dry jar and keep in a cool place.

About 2 hours before serving, heat the grill to its hottest setting. Sprinkle the powdered caramel evenly over the surface of the custards and put them under the grill about 5 cm (2 inches) away from the heat. Grill for 2–3 minutes until the caramel melts. Chill again until ready to serve.

COOK'S TIPS
* The custards can be made up to 1 day ahead and kept in the fridge. The powdered caramel can be made up to 3 days ahead.
* The strawberry sauce is frozen to prevent it from rising up into the custard mixture.
* Making a powdered caramel makes life easier. It's simpler and faster to get an even caramel topping on the custards.

Gather all the glitter and gold needed to create gorgeous Christmas cards and labels

Chocolate Cherry Drizzle Cake

Topped with luscious curls of chocolate, this rich chocolate cake looks amazing and tastes sensational with its sweet cherry and orange filling.

Makes 12–14 slices

ingredients

400 g (14 oz) Bonne Maman
  Cherry Compote
400 g (14 oz) milk chocolate,
  roughly chopped
200 g (7 oz) unsalted butter
90 g (3½ oz) self-raising flour
90 g (3½ oz) plain flour
¼ tsp bicarbonate of soda
200 g (7 oz) light muscovado
  sugar
200 g (7 oz) golden caster sugar
25 g (1 oz) cocoa powder
Grated zest and juice of 1 small
  orange
3 eggs
75 ml (3 fl oz) natural yogurt
2 tbsp Grand Marnier
275 ml (9 fl oz) double cream
Grated chocolate or chocolate
  curls, to decorate

method

Sit a large sieve over a bowl and tip in the cherry compote. Leave to drain for 2 hours.

Preheat the oven to 170°C (fan oven 150°C), gas mark 3. Line a deep, 18–20 cm (7–8 inch) cake tin with non-stick baking parchment.

Put 200 g (7 oz) of the chocolate into a saucepan and add the butter with 125 ml (4 fl oz) cold water. Place over a low heat until melted.

Mix the dry ingredients in a large bowl and stir in the orange zest, melted chocolate, eggs and yogurt. Pour this into the lined cake tin and bake in the preheated oven for 1½ hours or until a skewer pushed into the centre comes out clean. Leave to cool in the tin.

Pour the drained compote liquid into a small saucepan with the orange juice and Grand Marnier. Bring to the boil and bubble until reduced to about 6 tablespoons. Leave to cool.

Put the remaining chocolate into a saucepan, add 2 tablespoons of the reduced cherry liquid and the double cream. Leave over a low heat until the chocolate has melted. Stir until smooth, then cover and chill the cherry ganache for 30 minutes.

Cut the cake into 3 layers. Drizzle the bottom layer with some of the remaining cherry liquid, spread with a quarter of the ganache and scatter over half of the drained cherries. Sandwich the second layer on top and repeat with the remaining cherry liquid, another quarter of the ganache and the rest of the cherries. Top with the final layer, spread the remaining ganache over the top of the cake and decorate with grated chocolate or chocolate curls.

Raspberry and Chocolate Fudge Pots

Sweet and gooey chocolate fudge mixed with tart raspberries is the perfect antidote to a cold winter's day.

Serves 6

ingredients

50 g (2 oz) butter, plus extra for greasing
150 g (5 oz) milk chocolate
50 g (2 oz) dark, good-quality chocolate (70% cocoa solids)
1 tbsp chocolate hazelnut spread
100 g (3½ oz) golden caster sugar
3 large eggs, separated
6 tbsp fresh orange juice
6 tbsp orange-flavoured liqueur, such as Cointreau
12 level tbsp Bonne Maman Raspberry Conserve

to serve

Icing sugar, to dust
Double or single cream

method

Preheat the oven to 200°C (fan oven 180°C), gas mark 6. Lightly butter 6 ovenproof cups or deep ramekins.

Break the chocolate into a heatproof bowl and melt over a pan of gently simmering water (do not allow the base of the bowl to touch the water). Leave for 10–12 minutes, or until the chocolate has completely melted.

Dice the butter and drop it into the warm chocolate with the chocolate spread and leave to melt.

Meanwhile, put the sugar into a large bowl with the egg yolks and beat well until thick, pale and creamy.

Stir the chocolate mixture until smooth, then gently fold it into the creamed sugar and yolks.

Stir the orange juice and liqueur into the conserve and spoon into the bottom of each buttered cup.

Whisk the egg whites until they form soft peaks and quickly fold them into the chocolate mixture. Gently spoon this into the cups over the conserve.

Put the cups in a roasting tin and add enough boiling water to come about 2.5 cm (1 inch) up the sides of the cups. Bake in the preheated oven for 20–25 minutes or until the tops are risen and quite firm to the touch. The centres will still be wobbly with a delectable hot raspberry sauce beneath.

Serve these fudge pots hot, dusted with icing sugar; warm with a generous dollop of well-chilled extra thick cream or cold with chilled single cream.

Cinnamon and Strawberry Meringues

Everyone loves meringues when they're crispy on the outside and soft and mallow within – just like these! Served simply with softly whipped cream and strawberry conserve, they are quite irresistible.

Makes 12 meringues

ingredients

200 g (7 oz) egg whites, about 6 or 7 large eggs
265 g (9½ oz) golden caster sugar
140 g (4½ oz) light brown muscovado sugar
½ tsp ground cinnamon
12 generous tbsp Bonne Maman Strawberry and Wild Strawberry Conserve
1 x 300 ml carton double cream, lightly whipped
A few sliced strawberries
Icing sugar, to dust

method

Preheat the oven to 150°C (fan oven 130°C), gas mark 2.

Put the egg whites and sugars in a large heatproof bowl and sit it over a pan of gently simmering water. Leave for 7–10 minutes, stirring occasionally, until the mixture gets quite warm and the sugar has completely dissolved into the egg whites.

Transfer the mixture to the bowl of an electric mixer and beat the egg whites until they are very firm, shiny and cold. This can be done with a hand-held electric whisk but it does take a good 8–10 minutes.

Line 2 baking sheets with non-stick baking parchment, sticking the corners down with a little bit of the meringue mixture. Use 2 large basting spoons to lift 12 dollops of meringue onto the sheets and fork up into spikes. Sprinkle generously with cinnamon.

Bake the meringues in the preheated oven for about 1–1½ hours. When you lift one up it should feel dry on top but mallowy when you press against the base. Leave to cool on a wire rack.

To serve, gently push the base of the meringues inwards with the back of a spoon to create a hollow. Fill with conserve and a tablespoon of the cream. Sit the meringues upright on individual serving plates and add an extra spoonful of cream, topped with some sliced strawberries and a dusting of icing sugar.

COOK'S TIPS

* Keep the meringues in an airtight container for up to 4 days. Once filled, the meringues will keep in the fridge for up to 3 hours.
* Try using half light muscovado sugar and half dark muscovado sugar for a rich 'toffee' flavour to the meringues.
* Make 24 smaller meringues and sandwich together traditionally with the cream or whisk 4 tablespoons of Bonne Maman Confiture de Caramel into the whipped cream before using.

French Macaroons with Salted Nut Caramel

Delightful macaroons are appearing in every smart pâtisserie window. Bite into these macaroons and enjoy the sweetness of the toffee with a hint of almond and peanut and finally the tingle of salt.

Makes about 12–15

ingredients

125 g (4 oz) ground almonds
250 g (9 oz) icing sugar
3 egg whites
8 g sachet dried egg white
  powder
25 g (1 oz) caster sugar
Dessicated coconut, for
  sprinkling (optional)

for the filling

5 tbsp Bonne Maman Confiture
  de Caramel
2 tbsp smooth peanut butter
25 g (1 oz) shelled pistachio
  nuts, finely chopped

method

Preheat the oven to 190°C (fan oven 170°C), gas mark 5. Line 2–3 baking sheets with non-stick baking parchment and set aside.

Place the ground almonds and icing sugar together in the bowl of a food processor or blender and whizz together for about 5 seconds.

Put the egg whites and dried egg white powder into a large, clean bowl and whisk together until they form stiff peaks. Gradually whisk in the caster sugar until the mixture is very thick and shiny.

With a large metal spoon, quickly fold the almond and icing sugar into the meringue until evenly blended.

Spoon the mixture into a piping bag fitted with a 1 cm (½ inch) nozzle. Pipe rounds about 3.5 cm (1½ inch) in diameter onto the lined baking sheets, leaving the same amount of space between each one. You should get at least 30 rounds. Sprinkle with a little dessicated coconut if wished. Set them aside for 15 minutes to allow the macaroons to form a crust on top.

Bake in the preheated oven for about 5 minutes or until the base has set. Then, using a palette knife, gently ease the macaroons off the paper and flip them over to bake the underside. Bake for a further 5 minutes, then leave to cool on a wire rack.

Meanwhile, make the filling. Beat together the confiture de caramel and peanut butter. Sandwich the macaroons with the caramel mixture, spreading it right to the edge of the rounds. Finally, roll the filled macaroons in chopped pistachio nuts. Eat within 2 hours.

COOK'S TIPS

* If you don't like peanut butter, beat enough confiture de caramel into 75 g (3 oz) mascarpone cheese to form a smooth, spreadable consistency. Sandwich the macaroons and roll them in toasted desiccated coconut.
* Instead of piping the mixture, it is possible to drop even spoonfuls into rough rounds on the baking sheets. They won't have the dainty look of piped ones but will taste just as good and have a charm of their own!

Sticky Rhubarb and Syrup Puddings

A sticky rhubarb, orange and golden syrup sauce soaks into these light steamed sponges. Perfect for Sunday lunch but special enough to serve to friends for supper.

Serves 6–8

ingredients

175 g (6 oz) softened butter, plus extra for greasing
175 g (6 oz) golden caster sugar
175 g (6 oz) self-raising flour
1 tsp baking powder
4 eggs, beaten
2–3 tbsp soured cream or milk
Finely grated zest of 1 small orange
Chilled custard or cream, to finish

for the syrup

100 ml (3½ fl oz) Bonne Maman Rhubarb Compote
100 ml (3½ fl oz) golden syrup
100 ml (3½ fl oz) fresh orange juice
1 small orange, very thinly sliced

method

Preheat the oven to 180°C (fan oven 160°C), gas mark 4. Generously butter 8 x 175–200 ml (6–7 fl oz) metal pudding basins.

Put the sugar and butter together in a large bowl and, with an electric whisk (mixer or hand-held), beat together until very light and fluffy.

Add all the remaining sponge ingredients and continue to whisk for a further 2–3 minutes until the mixture is very smooth and creamy.

Spoon this into the prepared basins and level the top. Cover each one with buttered foil, butter side down with the edges sealed tightly around the top of the basins.

Put the basins in a large roasting tin and fill with enough boiling water to come halfway up the side of the basins. Steam in the preheated oven for about 1–1¼ hours.

Meanwhile make the syrup. Put the compote, golden syrup and orange juice in a wide, shallow pan and stir over a gentle heat until the syrup has melted.

Add the orange slices to the pan in a single layer and bring the liquid to the boil. Reduce the heat and simmer the slices very gently for about 15–20 minutes until the peel is tender and translucent, and the liquid has thickened to a syrupy consistency. Carefully remove the orange slices to a plate using a slotted spoon and set aside.

Loosen the edges of the hot puddings with a round bladed knife and turn out onto individual edged dishes. Spoon over the warm rhubarb syrup and add an orange slice on top. Finish with chilled custard or single cream.

COOK'S TIP

* If you would rather make 1 large sponge, spoon the mixture into a greased 1.1 litre (2 pint) pudding basin. Take a large sheet of foil and make a pleat down the centre. Butter well and use to cover the basin, butter side down. Fold the edges under to seal well. Put the pudding in a large, deep saucepan and pour in boiling water to come halfway up the sides. Cover with a lid or foil and simmer gently for about 2–2¼ hours. Keep an eye on the level of the water and add more as necessary.

A beautiful Christmas centrepiece.

Spiced Apricot and Carrot Cake

The quality of carrot cakes varies enormously but this one is light and moist with a delicate flavour of spices and apricots. It would make a wonderful alternative to traditional Christmas fruit cake.

Serves 10–12

ingredients

1 x 600 g jar Bonne Maman Apricot Compote
300 g (11 oz) dark soft brown sugar
3 large eggs
225 ml (7½ fl oz) sunflower oil
200 g (7 oz) self-raising wholemeal flour
100 g (3½ oz) self-raising flour
75 g (3 oz) desiccated coconut
1½ tsp bicarbonate of soda
4 tsp ground mixed spice
250 g (9 oz) carrots, peeled and coarsely grated

for the icing

Juice of 1 small lemon and 1–2 tangerines
250 g (9 oz) mascarpone cheese

method

Empty the jar of compote into a mesh sieve over a bowl and spread out the fruit. Leave to drain for 2 hours, stirring occasionally.

Preheat the oven to 170°C (fan oven 150°C), gas mark 3. Line the base and sides of a 20 cm (8 inch) round, 10 cm (4 inch) deep cake tin with non-stick baking parchment.

With a hand-held electric whisk, beat together 250 g (9 oz) of the sugar with the eggs and oil for 3–4 minutes. Stir in all the remaining cake ingredients until evenly mixed and spoon into the prepared tin.

Bake for about 2 hours or until golden brown and firm to the touch. A skewer pushed into the centre should come out clean.

Meanwhile, put the drained apricot compote liquid into a measuring jug (there should be 300 ml (½ pint) – make up to 300 ml (½ pint) with tangerine juice if necessary) and stir in the remaining dark brown sugar, lemon and tangerine juice.

Leave the cooked cake to cool in the tin for 15 minutes before turning out onto a wire rack. Cut in half and pierce the cake all over with a skewer. Spoon about 5 tablespoons of the sweetened juice over each of the cut surfaces. Leave to soak and cool.

Put the mascarpone in a bowl and beat in enough of the remaining sweetened juice to give a smooth, spreadable consistency. Do this gradually, beating in about 2–3 tablespoons at a time. The mascarpone should look like lightly whipped cream.

Spread 1 large tablespoon of mascarpone icing over the cut side of the top of the cake. Spread the drained fruit on top. Cover with what was the base of the cake (which is the flattest) and spread the remaining icing all over the top and sides of the cake. Keep in a cool place, preferably the fridge, and use within 1 week.

COOK'S TIPS

* The finished cake will freeze for up to 3 months. Thaw overnight in the fridge, then allow 10–15 minutes at room temperature before serving.
* For added decoration, toast some large flakes of coconut or extra desiccated coconut and sprinkle over the top of the cake.

Chocolate and Caramel Tart

This is the most heavenly combination: creamy chocolate caramel mousse over a caramel and hazelnut paste and finished with a thin chocolate icing. Although there are a few stages, the finished tart freezes so it can be made ahead and it is well worth the effort.

Serves 8–10

ingredients

1 x 400 g pack chilled shortcrust
    pastry
4 eggs
150 g (5 oz) unsalted butter
50 g (2 oz) hazelnuts, toasted
    and finely chopped
40 g (1½ oz) stoned soft dates,
    finely chopped
1 rounded tsp plain flour
50 g (2 oz) light soft brown
    sugar
1 x 380 g jar Bonne Maman
    Confiture de Caramel
200 g (7 oz) plain or milk
    chocolate
50 g (2 oz) caster sugar
Finely grated zest of ½ orange
6 tbsp double cream

method

Preheat the oven to 200°C (fan oven 180°C), gas mark 6.

Line a 23 cm (9 inch), deep loose-bottomed tart tin with rolled out pastry. Chill for 30 minutes, then bake blind (see page 41) in the preheated oven for 15–20 minutes until it is just beginning to colour round the edges.

Beat 1 of the eggs and use it to brush the cooked pastry all over. Return to the oven for 2–3 minutes and this will seal the pastry and prevent any leaks.

Melt 25 g (1 oz) of butter and mix with the remaining beaten egg, hazelnuts, dates, flour, light soft brown sugar and 50 g (2 oz) of the caramel.

Spoon over the base of the pastry case and return the tin to the oven for 25–30 minutes or until just set. Leave to cool.

To make the mousse, place 150 g (5 oz) of the chocolate in a heatproof bowl over a pan of gently simmering water. When melted, remove from the heat and add 100 g (3½ oz) of the butter and 50 g (2 oz) of the caramel.

Separate the remaining eggs and beat the yolks into the chocolate mixture. Whisk the egg whites to a soft peak, whisk in the caster sugar and continue to whisk until stiff. Fold into the chocolate along with the orange zest and spoon onto the cooked hazelnut paste. Smooth with a knife and chill overnight to set.

For the final icing, melt the remaining chocolate as above and stir in the remaining butter. Add 8 teaspoons confiture de caramel and the double cream and mix thoroughly. Pour the icing onto the chilled mousse and spread to the edges. Chill until needed.

COOK'S TIPS

* The tart can be made up to 2 days ahead and kept lightly covered in the fridge. Alternatively, you can freeze the tart. Thaw overnight at a cool room temperature.
* When making the chocolate mousse, put the bowl of melted chocolate on the scales, adjust to zero and measure the caramel straight into it.
* The chocolate and caramel mousse mixture is delicious on its own. Spoon into individual glass dishes and chill for about 2 hours to set. Spoon the chocolate icing over the top and chill again to set. Decorate with chocolate curls.

Bitter Orange Marmalade Muffins

These citrusy little muffins are perfect for breakfast or brunch and will bring a touch of sunshine to any dark and dingy winter's morning.

Makes 12

ingredients

175 g (6 oz) Bonne Maman
 Bitter Orange Marmalade
250 g (9 oz) self-raising flour
25 g (1 oz) bran
1 tbsp caster sugar
50 g (2 oz) runny honey
2 tbsp baking powder
½ tsp ground cinnamon
4 tbsp vegetable oil
1 large egg
125 g (4 oz) raisins
125 ml (4 fl oz) orange juice
1 tbsp wheatgerm

method

Preheat the oven to 190°C (fan oven 170°C), gas mark 5. Fill a 12-hole muffin tin with muffin cases.

Place all of the ingredients except the wheatgerm into a bowl and mix together with a spoon until combined.

Fill each muffin case three-quarters full with the muffin mixture and sprinkle with the wheatgerm.

Bake on a centre shelf in the preheated oven for about 25–30 minutes.

COOK'S TIPS

* Omit the raisins and use dried cherries or chopped dried apricots.
* The muffins are best eaten within 2 days or they can be cooked and frozen. To use, thaw overnight and warm in a low oven for 5–10 minutes.

Strawberry and Orange Polenta Cake

This fresh and fruity cake with a citrus punch and a sticky hot strawberry drizzle over the top, makes a delicious tea-time treat.

Serves 8–10

ingredients

150 ml (¼ pint) blood orange juice
8 tbsp Bonne Maman Strawberry Conserve
3 small oranges, thinly sliced
50 g (2 oz) self-raising flour
150 g (5 oz) ground almonds
150 g (5 oz) polenta
1 tsp baking powder
200 g (7 oz) unsalted butter
200 g (7 oz) golden caster sugar
3 eggs, beaten
Finely grated zest and juice of 1 orange
1 tsp vanilla extract
2 tsp poppy seeds
50 ml (2 fl oz) vodka (optional)
Crème fraîche, to finish

method

Preheat the oven to 180°C (fan oven 160°C), gas mark 4. Line the base and sides of a 20 cm (8 inch) springform cake tin with greaseproof paper.

Put the blood orange juice and 6 tablespoons of the conserve in a large frying pan with 150 ml (¼ pint) water. Bring to the boil, stirring, until the conserve has melted.

Add the orange slices in an even layer and simmer gently for 10–15 minutes or until the slices are translucent and soft. Lift the slices from the pan using a slotted spoon and use them to line the base and sides of the cake tin. Reserve the poaching liquid.

Mix together the flour, almonds, polenta and baking powder in a mixing bowl. Beat together the butter and sugar until very pale and creamy in a separate large bowl. Gradually beat in the eggs, adding a spoonful of the dry ingredients between each addition.

Fold in the remaining dry ingredients with the orange zest, juice, vanilla essence and poppy seeds.

Spoon the cake mixture into the tin and level the surface. Bake in the preheated oven for 30 minutes. Reduce the oven temperature to 170°C (fan oven 150°C), gas mark 3 and continue to bake for a further 25 minutes or until a skewer pushed into the centre comes out clean.

Meanwhile, stir the remaining 2 tablespoons of conserve into the reserved poaching liquid and bring to the boil. Bubble for 5–7 minutes or until the liquid is reduced to a sticky syrup. Stir in the vodka, if using, and set aside.

Turn the cake out onto a wire rack to cool. Brush or spoon over about half the strawberry syrup until all the orange slices are glazed.

Serve in wedges with the remaining syrup and a generous spoonful of crème fraîche.

Berries and Cherries Verrines with Cinnamon Crackle

Verrines are little layered pots, a little similar to our trifle, that have been popular in France for many years. Once the 'crackle' is made, these are very quick to assemble.

Serves 6

ingredients

1 x 150 ml carton double cream
½ tsp vanilla extract
1 tbsp caster sugar
1 x 200 ml tub crème fraîche
8 generous tbsp Bonne Maman Berries and Cherries Conserve
2 tbsp Kirsch, Grand Marnier, Cointreau, vodka or pomegranate juice

for the cinnamon 'crackle'

1 tsp bicarbonate of soda
A large pinch of ground cinnamon
150 g (5 oz) golden caster sugar
100 g (3½ oz) golden syrup
1 tbsp white wine vinegar
50 g (2 oz) chopped walnut pieces, toasted

method

First make the 'crackle'. Line a small baking sheet with non-stick baking parchment. Mix together the bicarbonate of soda and cinnamon.

Put the sugar, syrup, vinegar and 75 ml (3 fl oz) cold water in a medium saucepan and heat gently, stirring, until the sugar has dissolved completely. Cover the pan and simmer for 2 minutes, then remove the lid and bubble the mixture until it turns golden brown.

Very quickly stir in the bicarbonate of soda mixture (it will bubble) and pour onto the baking sheet. Scatter the walnuts on top and leave to cool. Break into rough chunks and set aside.

Lightly whisk the double cream with the vanilla and sugar until it just begins to hold its shape, then fold into the crème fraîche. Mix together the conserve and liqueur or juice.

Just before serving, layer the cinnamon 'crackle' with the conserve and cream in pretty glasses. Finish with a few powdery pieces of 'crackle'.

COOK'S TIPS

* The cinnamon 'crackle' can be made up to 2 days ahead and kept in an airtight container. Mix the conserve with the liqueur or juice the day before and keep in the fridge.
* If you don't want to make the crackle, buy 3–4 x 40 g (1½ oz) chocolate-covered honeycomb bars and roughly chop.

Apricot Mince Pies

Full of the flavours of Christmas, these special mince pies will be enjoyed throughout the festive season and beyond.

Makes 12

ingredients

100 g (3 ½ oz) unsalted butter, at room temperature and cubed, plus extra for greasing
200 g (7 oz) plain flour, plus extra for dusting
1 tsp ground mixed spice
1 tbsp caster sugar
6 tsp Bonne Maman Apricot Conserve
6 tsp good-quality mincemeat
Milk or beaten egg, for glazing
Icing sugar, to dust

method

Preheat the oven to 200°C (fan oven 180°C), gas mark 6. Lightly grease a 12-hole cake tin.

Put the flour into a mixing bowl, add the butter and rub into the flour until the mixture is like fine breadcrumbs.

Add the mixed spice to the sugar in a pestle and mortar or a strong bowl with the end of a rolling pin and grind together until well mixed and a little powdery. Add this to the flour and butter and stir in.

Using a round-bladed palette knife, mix in 3–4 tablespoons cold water, stirring until it comes together. Then with your hands, work the dough gently into a ball, wrap in cling film and allow to rest for about 20 minutes.

Roll out the pastry thinly on a lightly floured work surface. Stamp out 12 circles with a fluted pastry cutter, slightly larger than the cake holes, and press the circles into the tin.

Put about ½ teaspoon of apricot conserve into each pastry case, then top with about ½ teaspoon of mincemeat.

Re-roll the pastry trimmings and cut out 12 smaller circles and put them on top of the mincemeat. Glaze the tops with a little milk or beaten egg, if available, and bake in the preheated oven for 12–15 minutes until the pastry is crisp and golden.

Cool in the tin for 5 minutes, then remove and cool on a wire rack. Dust with icing sugar to finish.

Seasonal gifts

Making your own presents is one of the most loving ways of giving at Christmas and one of the most appreciated too.

Fill Bonne Maman jars with homemade fudge, pale green peppermint creams, a variety of sweets, little star-shaped biscuits, spiced nuts and other seasonal treats, decorate the pretty lids with co-ordinating ribbons and yuletide-themed trimmings, and create some beautifully personalised labels to make your gifts extra special.

Christmas Cherry Soufflé

Wondering what to do with the last morsel of Christmas pudding? Despite its myriad of rich flavours – Christmas pudding, ginger, cherries and brandy – this soufflé manages to taste decadent yet light.

Serves 2–3

ingredients

- 40 g (1½ oz) butter, plus extra for greasing
- 25 g (1 oz) cold Christmas pudding, crumbled
- 2 tbsp brandy
- 25 g (1 oz) Bonne Maman Black Cherry Conserve
- 4 tbsp plain flour
- 300 ml (½ pint) whole milk
- 75 g (3 oz) golden caster sugar
- 25 g (1 oz) stem ginger, finely chopped
- 4 large eggs, separated
- Icing sugar, to dust

method

Preheat the oven to 180°C (fan oven 160°C), gas mark 4. Butter an 18 cm (7 inch), 1.7 litre (3 pint) soufflé dish. Put a flat baking sheet in the oven to heat up.

Stir together the crumbled Christmas pudding with the brandy and conserve and set aside.

Melt the butter in a saucepan, stir in the flour and gradually add the milk. Bring to the boil, stirring, then reduce the heat and cook for 2 minutes. Stir in 50 g (2 oz) of the sugar with the ginger, then beat in the egg yolks. Gently fold the Christmas pudding mixture into the sauce.

Whisk the egg whites until they form soft peaks, then gradually whisk in the remaining sugar until the meringue is stiff and glossy. With a large metal spoon fold the meringue into the sauce and turn into the prepared dish.

Sit the dish on the heated baking sheet and bake for 45 minutes until well risen and golden. Dust with icing sugar and serve straight away.

COOK'S TIPS

* The sauce for the soufflé can be made the day before it is needed. Don't beat in the 50 g (2 oz) sugar but sprinkle on top of the sauce to prevent a skin forming. When ready to cook, beat well before whisking and fold in the meringue as above.
* Buttering the dish helps the soufflé to rise up in the oven.
* Omit the ginger and add a pinch of mixed spice to the pudding mixture.
* Serve with chilled cream or vanilla ice cream if liked.

les petites astuces
hints and tips

Spring

Make a creamy cheese frosting for carrot cake by beating enough Bonne Maman Bitter Orange Marmalade and a large pinch of ground cinnamon into a 200 g pack mascarpone cheese until spreadable.

Mix 4 tablespoons Bonne Maman Blackcurrant Conserve with 2 tablespoons balsamic vinegar and 1 tablespoon chopped fresh mint for a fruity alternative to mint jelly for new season's lamb.

Whisk a spoonful of Bonne Maman Apricot Compote into mayonnaise with some curry paste and crushed garlic. Delicious served with cold roast chicken.

When frying steaks or duck breasts, stir 1 tablespoon Bonne Maman Black Cherry Conserve into the pan juices with a splash of port or red wine. Bubble for 1–2 minutes, scraping the pan with a wooden spoon. Add a squeeze of lemon and pour over the steaks.

Try Bitter Orange Marmalade layered into bread and butter pudding to give a tangy zest to an old favourite.

Summer

Make a syrup for a fruit salad by mixing 4 tablespoons Bonne Maman Strawberry Conserve with 300 ml (½ pint) red grape juice and the pulp of 2 passion fruit. Strain over the fruit and chill for about 1 hour.

At the height of summer, make some blueberry lemonade: put 200 ml (7 fl oz) fresh lemon juice, 400 ml (14 fl oz) water and a 370 g jar Bonne Maman Wild Blueberry Conserve in a blender. Whizz until mixed, then strain into a jug half-filled with ice and serve.

Put a spoonful of conserve in the base of waffle cones to save ice cream drips.

Mix up a great barbecue baste by beating 4 tablespoons Bonne Maman Blackcurrant Conserve with 1 tablespoon Dijon mustard, 2 tablespoons white wine vinegar, 2 tablespoons tomato ketchup and some crushed garlic.

Try a tasty basil dressing to spoon over roasted summer vegetables by putting 25 g (1 oz) fresh basil in a blender with the zest and juice of 1 small lemon, 4 tablespoons olive oil, 1 garlic clove and 1 tablespoon Bonne Maman Fig Conserve. Blitz until blended.

For an instant rhubarb fool, stir Bonne Maman Rhubarb Compote into an equal mix of whipped cream and thick Greek yogurt. Top with pistachio nuts.

Autumn

Core and stuff cooking apples with chopped dried figs, Bonne Maman Confiture de Caramel and a little butter and cinnamon. Then bake in the oven for about an hour. A little water in the dish keeps them moist.

Make simple autumn verrines. Divide 50 g (2 oz) crushed amaretti biscuits between 4 small glass dishes. Pour over 2 tablespoons brandy and scatter 4 sliced fresh figs and 4 sliced fresh apricots on top. Spoon over 300 g (11 oz) Bonne Maman Apricot Compote, add a layer of Greek yogurt and chill until ready to serve.

Enjoy porridge with a spoonful of Bonne Maman Cherry Compote, a spoonful of honey and a pinch of ground cinnamon to add extra flavour.

If you have run out of mango chutney, mix together some Bonne Maman Apricot Conserve with a squeeze of lime juice and a little chopped red chilli.

Don't throw away the soft apples from the fruit bowl: peel, core and chop them into some Bonne Maman Rhubarb Compote and add grated fresh ginger. Simmer until soft, then serve warm with pork or duck.

Winter

For a party nibble, toss 450 g (1 lb) cocktail chipolata sausages with a mix of 1 tablespoon mango chutney, 1 tablespoon Bonne Maman Apricot Conserve and 1 tablespoon wholegrain mustard. Roast in a hot oven until golden brown and sticky, turning occasionally.

When making tomato-based sauces and soups with tinned tomatoes, add 1 teaspoon Bonne Maman Blackcurrant Conserve to bring out the sweetness of the tomatoes.

To glaze a Christmas gammon, brush the fat with equal quantities of Dijon mustard and Bonne Maman Apricot or Peach Conserve. Stud with 2 or 3 whole cloves or star anise and roast in a hot oven for 10–15 minutes.

Stir a spoonful of Bonne Maman Mandarin Marmalade into cranberry sauce for a delicious hint of orange.

All seasons

To make a delicious version of French toast, sandwich 2 slices of buttered bread with Bonne Maman Conserve, cut into fingers, dip in beaten egg with a drop of vanilla extract and fry till golden and crisp.

For a quick taste of banoffee, fold sliced banana and crushed digestive biscuits into a pot of full-fat Greek yogurt and add some Bonne Maman Confiture de Caramel for that fudgy taste.

When making hot vanilla custard, cut the amount of sugar by 25 g (1 oz) and stir in 2 tablespoons Bonne Maman Apricot or Peach Conserve just before serving.

Mix together 2 tablespoons Bonne Maman Confiture de Caramel with a 150 ml carton single cream and

warm gently. Serve with apple pie, baked apples or poached pears.

Make a simple trifle by replacing the fruit with some Bonne Maman Apricot Compote spooned over chopped lemon drizzle cake and topped with custard and whipped cream as usual.

When making a classic lemon tart brush the base of the cooked pastry with 2–3 tablespoons Bonne Maman Raspberry Conserve or Jelly and continue as usual.

If you add too much chilli to a curry try adding a spoonful of Bonne Maman Apricot or Peach Conserve. A little added sweetness will mellow some of the heat.

Asian recipes often require palm sugar, but you can substitute Bonne Maman Confiture de Caramel. It has a similar rich fudgy flavour.

The Spanish like to serve sweet quince paste with their cheese; a delicious alternative is to offer a small pot of Bonne Maman Fig Conserve with a cheese board of fresh goats' and strong blue-veined cheeses.

Index

Conversion tables

The tables below are only approximate and are meant to be used as a guide only.

Approximate American/European conversions

	USA	Metric	Imperial
brown sugar	1 cup	175 g	6 oz
butter	1 stick	125 g	4 oz
butter/margarine/lard	1 cup	225 g	8 oz
caster and granulated sugar	2 level tablespoons	25 g	1 oz
caster and granulated sugar	1 cup	225 g	8 oz
currants	1 cup	150 g	5 oz
flour	1 cup	150 g	5 oz
golden syrup	1 cup	350 g	12 oz
ground almonds	1 cup	125 g	4 oz
sultanas/raisins	1 cup	200 g	7 oz

Approximate American/European conversions

American	European
1 teaspoon	1 teaspoon/5 ml
½ fl oz	1 tablespoon/½ fl oz/15 ml
¼ cup	4 tablespoons/2 fl oz/50 ml
½ cup plus 2 tablespoons	¼ pint/5 fl oz/150 ml
1¼ cups	½ pint/10 fl oz/300 ml
1 pint/16 fl oz	1 pint/20 fl oz/600 ml
2½ pints (5 cups)	1.1 litres/2 pints
10 pints	4.5 litres/8 pints

Liquid measures

Imperial	ml	fl oz
1 teaspoon	5	
2 tablespoons	25	1
4 tablespoons	50	2
¼ pint/1 gill	150	5
⅓ pint	200	7
½ pint	300	10
¾ pint	450	15
1 pint	600	20
1¾ pints	1000 (1 litre)	35

Oven temperatures

American	Celsius	Fahrenheit	Gas Mark
Cool	130	250	½
Very slow	140	275	1
Slow	150	300	2
Moderate	170	325	3
Moderate	180	350	4
Moderately hot	190	375	5
Fairly hot	200	400	6
Hot	220	425	7
Very hot	230	450	8
Extremely hot	240	475	9

Other useful measurements

Measurement	Metric	Imperial
1 American cup	225 ml	7½ fl oz
1 egg, size 3	50 ml	2 fl oz
1 egg white	25 ml	1 fl oz
1 rounded tablespoon flour	25 g	1 oz
1 rounded tablespoon cornflour	25 g	1 oz
1 rounded tablespoon caster sugar	25 g	1 oz
2 level teaspoons gelatine	10 g	¼ oz

AGA conversion – oven temperature to heat

Temperature		2 oven Aga	3 oven Aga	4 oven Aga
°C	Gas mark			
240	9	Roasting Oven	Roasting Oven	Roasting Oven
230	8	Middle Roasting Oven	Middle Roasting Oven	Middle Roasting Oven
220	7	Lower Roasting Oven	Lower Roasting Oven	Lower Roasting Oven
200	6	Grid shelf on floor of Roasting Oven	Grid shelf on floor of Roasting Oven	Grid shelf on floor of Roasting Oven
190	5	Grid shelf on floor of Roasting Oven	Top of Baking Oven	Top of Baking Oven
180	4	Grid shelf on floor of Roasting Oven with cold plain shelf on second runners	Middle of Baking Oven	Middle of Baking Oven
160	3	Grid shelf on floor of Roasting Oven with cold plain shelf on third runners	Grid shelf on floor of Baking Oven	Grid shelf on floor of Baking Oven
150	2	Simmering Oven	Simmering Oven	Simmering Oven
140	1	Simmering Oven	Simmering Oven	Simmering Oven
130	½	Simmering Oven with cold plain shelf	Simmering Oven with cold plain shelf	Warming Oven
110			Warming Oven	
100				Warming Oven

Grill at the top of the Roasting Oven

Cook pizzas, pies and quiches in glass or ceramic dishes on the cast-iron floor of the Roasting Oven for good base browning.